PELICAN BOOKS

ON THE EXPERIENCE OF TIME

Robert E. Ornstein is a graduate of Queens College of the City University of New York and of Stanford University. He now teaches at the University of California Medical Center in San Francisco and is a research psychologist at The Langley Porter Neuropsychiatric Institute. In 1969 he received the American Institutes of Research Creative Talent Award. Professor Ornstein is author of *The Psychology of Consciousness,* also published by Penguin Books, and coauthor, with Claudio Naranjo, of *On the Psychology of Meditation.*

Robert E. Ornstein

On the Experience of Time

Penguin Books

Penguin Books Inc, 72 Fifth Avenue,
New York, New York 10011, U.S.A.
Penguin Books Inc, 7110 Ambassador Road,
Baltimore, Maryland 21207, U.S.A.
Penguin Books Ltd, Harmondsworth,
Middlesex, England
Penguin Books Australia Ltd, Ringwood,
Victoria, Australia
Penguin Books Canada Limited, 41 Steelcase Road West,
Markham, Ontario, Canada L3R 1B4
Penguin Books (N.Z.) Ltd, 182–190 Wairau Road,
Auckland 10, New Zealand

First published by Penguin Education
   in the Science of Behaviour Series, 1969
Published in Pelican Books, 1975

Copyright © Robert E. Ornstein, 1969

Printed in the United States of America

For Jeanne, David and Faith

Contents

Editorial Foreword

As Ornstein notes, everyone at some period in his life puzzles about the experience of time. I well remember devoting my thoughts to this problem one summer, a part of which I spent walking the back beach of Cape Cod in the style of Thoreau (but with feet bare). My conclusion at that time (some 15 years ago) was that I was unready to come to grips seriously with this enigma.

During 1967 and 1968, however, I was returned to the question specifically by my colleague Fred Melges, a psychiatrist with whom I had collaborated in thinking through the thicket we call emotions and feelings. Melges' main interest concerns time sense on which he has done a great deal of clinical observation and experimentation. We were wondering about a joint laboratory undertaking when an opportunity presented itself in the person of Charles Legg who wanted a post-doctoral experience after completing a thesis on time sense at Cambridge University. With Legg's arrival at Stanford we began to explore the time experience once again in earnest. The vehicle became my weekly noon seminars in neuropsychology. And through these we became acquainted with Bob Ornstein, who had been pursuing the problem elsewhere on campus. His views and the experiments he had accomplished hit a sympathetic cord in all of us but especially in me. The direction of research each of us had undertaken seemed to flow from some common assumptions and though the efforts of my laboratory had not been primarily directed to the problem of time experience, the results of our research appeared to have a great deal to say in support of Ornstein's formulation of the problem. The result of this interaction was my suggestion that Ornstein publish his manuscript and that the relevant neurological material be briefly summarized therein. This has been done (see pp. 49–51).

To me, Ornstein's approach to the analysis of the time experience makes eminent sense. Besides this, Ornstein's experiments are ingenious and his approach is fun to read about and to contemplate. Fun should be shared – so here is Ornstein on the 'experience of time'.

K. H. Pribram

Preface

I have always wondered about time. When I was younger I felt that I could understand most processes of perception, vision, hearing, etc. (If I had learned something about psychology then, I would not have been so smug.) But time? Where did it exist? In high school, a teacher encouraged me to read about Einstein and his ideas on time. I remember that it was Lincoln Barnett's *The Universe and Dr Einstein* which finally focused my awareness on time in psychology. From then on it was a problem which actively bothered me.

After a year or so's thought, the first experiment in this book was done. Since my thought process was not very coherent, I then jumped to another question – memory of time intervals. This direction was suggested by Dr Albert Hastorf of Stanford University, whose gentle prodding made it clear that I did have some more coherent ideas. I did the experiment which appears seventh in this series. The others were done in rapid succession once the idea of 'storage size' came clear. Until then, I had been quite reluctant to discuss or publish my work, since I am constitutionally predisposed to consider everything an open question like Barth's character Ebenezer. But I was continually reminded by Dr Hastorf that throwing one's hands up in the air was no solution to my questions and I was forced to make some sense (to myself, at least) of the vast evidence recorded about time experience. Once done, the experiments to be carried out were most clear. They were done in essentially random order, and then given some semblance of order by the writing. Probably no author has performed his experiments in the order in which they appear.

I have had the fortune of many collaborators. Dan Bernstein, who essentially did all the work on Experiments 3 and 4, was the first. Leah Light and two of her students did all the difficult and tedious planning and work on Experiment 2. E. Karim Sadalla and I discussed many of the experiments and collaborated on Experiment 6 as part of another project. Someday this project might be resumed. I have also greatly benefited from many discussions on psychology with Professor Sadalla.

Many other people have read and commented on the experiments and the manuscript. Foremost is Dr Hastorf who has patiently jibed me until I made my ideas clear. He also helped raise some of the problems which an analysis of time experience must treat. Drs Charles Hamilton and Alex Bavelas each took an active interest in my work and contributed many suggestions on both the actual experiments and the writing. The statistics in the latter experiments were learned from Dr Merrill Carlsmith, also of Stanford University.

So many others have read versions of the manuscript that I wonder who is left to buy the book. Among them are William Dement, Joe Kamiya, Karl Pribram, Charles Legg (who lent me a copy of his Ph.D. thesis to crib from), Enoch Callaway, David Galin, 'Petaluma' Charlie Furst, Beverly Timmons, J. T. Hart and Avram Miller. Each has made useful contributions. Surely with all these talented and concerned people aiding me with comments, any flaw which remains in the manuscript must be due to their collective oversight.

I would finally like to thank Miss Faith Hornbacher for designing and drawing the figures for Experiments 8 and 9 as well as providing help in setting up many of the experiments.

Much of the work was done while I held a National Institutes of Health Pre-Doctoral Fellowship at Stanford University, from 1965–8. Stanford also furnished the money for subjects, equipment, and space. A grant from the Janet Bickford Fund provided for the necessary secretarial expenses in the writing of the manuscript and xeroxing, postage, etc.

Robert Ornstein

1 The Probem of Temporal Experience

... One lies here with time passing and wonders about it. Every sort of time trickling through the hourglass, 'time immemorial', and 'for the time being', and 'time out of mind'; the time of the poet, the philosopher, the pregnant woman, the calendar ...

Lawrence Durrell, *Clea*

Time is one of the continuing, compelling and universal experiences of our lives, one of the primary threads which combine in the weave of our experience. All our perceptual, intellectual and emotional experiences are intertwined with time. We continually *feel* time passing but where does it come from? We continually experience it but we cannot taste it, see it, smell it, hear it or touch it. How, then, *do* we experience time? What do we *use* to experience it?

Each of us views time from our own particular vantage point. The poet, philosopher and psychologist try to explore the dimensions of our experience of time; the biologist and psychologist seek ways in which time might be experienced; the philosopher and psychologist view the ways in which time experiences reflect our world view. The physicist studies two times, the relativistic time of the universe and the molecular time of quantum mechanics. We have created hundreds of time 'keepers' from the burning of a candle, or of a rope tied in knots, to our common modern electric clock, calendar, sundial, hourglass or even the cesium clock.

This book is concerned with the times of ordinary experience, and particularly the experience of duration. Temporal experience, in its many forms, has been of continuing concern to psychologists and psychologically oriented philosophers since the time of the Greeks. Most of the great philosophers discussed their ideas of time experience and of time in physical science. As a rule, these ideas on the experience of time were applications of their general world views. Kant, for instance, held time to be an *a priori* construction of the mind (Kant, 1788), while Locke attempted to derive the experience of time from external occurrences, from 'the succession of ideas' (Locke, 1689), and Bergson stressed a relational subjective approach derived from the general ideas of relativity theory (Bergson, 1920).

When psychology began as the science of conscious experience, time was, naturally, one of the first experiences to be investigated. The early psychologists speculated at length on the nature of time. Titchener stressed an introspective view (Titchener, 1905), James tried to relate time to decay of 'brain traces' and to 'the multitudinousness of memories' (James, 1890), and Wundt and others tried to determine whether Weber's Law held for time (Woodrow, 1951).

Almost all the empirical work in this period was separate from the theoretical; experiments were performed on time experience in a large number of different situations. But there was little coherence in all of this empirical and theoretical work, save perhaps the work of Guyau (1890) which was an attempt to relate time experience to human information processing.

Nichols, in 1891, wrote the first review of time in psychology, sounding a theme which was to become the *leitmotif* of many reviews of time.

Casting an eye backward we can but be struck by the wide variety of explanations offered for the time-mystery. Time has been called an act of mind, of reason, of perception, of intuition, of sense, of memory, of will, of all possible compounds and compositions to be made up of them. It has been deemed a General Sense accompanying all mental content in a manner similar to that conceived of pain and pleasure. It has been assigned a separate, special, disparate sense, to nigh a dozen kinds of 'feeling', some familiar, some strangely invented for the difficulty. It has been explained by 'relations', by 'earmarks', by 'signs', by 'remnants', by 'struggles', and by 'strifes', by 'luminous trains', by 'blocks of specious-present', by 'apperception'. It has been declared *a priori*, innate, intuitive, empirical, mechanical. It has been deduced from within and without, from heaven, and from earth, and from several things difficult to imagine as of either (Nichols, 1891).

With a tributary of ideas so broad yet shallow it was not surprising that the mainstream of psychological thought began to draw less and less from the time literature. With Watson's (1924) purging of 'mentalism' from psychology, time's tributary almost dried up. The flow of research in perception as a whole began to abate but the work on time even more so. The reasons why time research has been and remains so scattered and so offensive to an 'objectively' minded psychology are clearly seen. For an analysis of the experience of time, one can point neither to an *organ* of perception, like the eye, nor to a physical continuum, like the wave-length of light for study by objective means. There is no immediate point of departure for a scientific analysis of time experience. One cannot immediately determine a process in the external world which gives rise to time experience, or discover anything within ourselves which could apprehend any special 'time stimuli'. It is, therefore, not too surprising that work on the experience of time would be so diverse, incoherent and easily forgotten.

Some have tried to overlook the lack of an organ of time, and have approached time experience as if it were a sensory process, as if we had a special 'time sense'. We often use the phrase a 'good sense of time' in ordinary speech to refer to someone who is accurate with respect to the clock, to someone who is 'on' time. This may be a useful everyday idea, but as a scientific concept it has seriously impeded an understanding of time experience. This will be discussed at length later in this chapter.

Returning to the chronology, it would be encouraging to find that work on time experience became more coherent in the 50 or 60 years following Nichols' scathing review. But the desire to be 'objective', in large part forced by Watson, made the 'time sense' approach easier to follow. If time was considered a 'sense' then it could at least be studied somewhat objectively, at least as objectively as vision. But there was no obvious point at which to begin. The organ of time was not as evident as the eye.

The empirical and theoretical research performed on time experience in this period (roughly 1890–1950) was marred by the same scattering as had taken place in the older philosophical literature. It seemed, again, as if each worker had his own special theoretical position or technical area of competence, and sought to relate his speciality to time experience. This resulted anew in several one-shot fragmentary research efforts. Blakey studied the 'time order error' (see Woodrow, 1934); Benussi, differences in coding a series of stimuli (Benussi, 1907); Harton, the effects of 'successful' and 'failure' experiences on time (Harton, 1939b, p. 51–62); Hoagland proposed a chemical theory of time experience based on his wife's tapping rate under a fever (Hoagland, 1933, 1935); Gardner studied the time experience of hyper- and hypo-thyroid patients, etc. (Gardner, 1935). Nichols could merely have added a few items to his 'time mystery' list if he had written 50 or 60 years later. The only researcher to make a continuing effort to understand time experience was Woodrow, who in 1951, summarized his work and that of others in this way:

The data that have been accumulated in the illusive field of time perception show two outstanding characteristics. One is the conflicting nature of the finding of the different experimenters, the other is the mentalistic nature of the data (Woodrow, 1951).

In spite of all this, the past 15 years has seen a considerable renewal of interest by psychologists in time experience, along with a general rebirth of concern with consciousness in psychology. Fraisse's *The Psychology of Time* (1963), a rather complete review of work of the last 75 years, probably sparked the interest, offering an historical review on which to build analyses of time experience. Frankenhaeuser (1959) also contributed a monograph and a beginning analysis of the cognitive determinants of time. Two new large volumes on time have recently appeared, Fraser's *The Voices of Time* (1966), and Fischer's *Interdisciplinary Perspectives of Time* (1967). These collections contain discussions of the multitude of time conceptions in literature, biology, religion, psychology, physics and in measurement. Along with these general indications, new systematic psychological experimentation is progressing in the analysis of the experience of brief intervals in the work of Michon (1967) and of Triesman (1963).

Yet Nichols' *leitmotif* persists to some. In 1964 Adams reviewed some of the time literature and wrote:

. . . time perception is a venerable, tired topic in psychology that interests very few active investigators any more, perhaps because no one bothered to explore the mechanisms of time perception and how [they] might enter into meaningful interaction with other mechanisms (Adams, 1964).

The intent of this work is to attempt to create some order out of the diverse data of time psychology, to integrate these data at a useful general level and to consider an hypothesis concerning the mechanism or class of mechanisms which underlie time experience, particularly that of duration. In short, I wish to try to help re-introduce an analysis of time experience back into the mainstream of research in perception and cognition, relating the experience of time to what is known of information processing, attention and memory. Michon has made a similar attempt in studying the rhythmic component of short time and I will try to do this for duration.

A first step towards obtaining a coherent picture of time experience would be to try to clarify the various different modes of time experience. Before doing this, we must keep in mind that the whole dimension of experiential time is but one form of time in general. There is a popular saying that 'time is money'. Time is not money, but the concept of time is similar to the concept of money in that each refer to many different sorts of things. Many distinct objects are used as 'money' but we would not confuse the English pound with two hundred sheep simply because either might be used as barter.

There are many forms of time. Gunn, in *The Problem of Time* (1929), points out that a stumbling block in physics has been the confusion of different time concepts, physical time with either mathematical time or with clock time. This has also been the case in psychology where the confusion has been between experiential time and either biological time or the clock of hours, minutes and seconds.

Experiments are often performed to determine how 'accurately' 'real' time is perceived. One of the first concerns of psychologists was how Weber's Law might fit time experience (Fraisse, 1963). Calling the clock of hours, minutes, and seconds 'real' time is like calling American money 'real money'. An analysis should be concerned with experiential time *per se*, not as it might relate to hours, days, burning rope or to some other time definition.

In analysing the experience of time we must distinguish between various distinct kinds of time experience, just as in the analysis of visual experience we separate colour from contour. As we ought be careful not to confuse experiential time with other time, we ought not confuse the different modes of time experience with one another.

It would be therefore useful to determine which research evidence bears on each different process, instead of lumping them all under the single heading of 'time sense'. It seems to me that there are four major varieties of time experience, the experience of very short interval – the present, the longer experience of duration, the experience of the future or of a temporal perspective, and the experience of simultaneity.

We continually experience the immediate present going by, the time that is always *now* (or just then *was* now). This is the time of our most immediate contact with the world, very short, continually changing, fading away, forever being replaced by a new *now*. Clay gave this the name of the 'specious present' (Clay, 1890). James quotes an anonymous poet describing it this way, 'the moment of which I speak is already far away' (James, 1890).

The idea of a fleeting, immediate present seems to have held up to more rigorous empirical analyses. Peterson and Peterson (1959) have demonstrated the existence of an immediate memory process, fleeting and decaying quickly, distinct from permanent memory. Miller (1956) showed that the information-processing capacity of this immediate memory is fixed at a low amount and is extremely difficult to modify by training. The clock time limits of this memory seem to vary, but for time *experience* we can say (along with Woodrow) that short-term time is around 3 or 4 s while long-term time or duration begins somewhere above 10 s. Several recent writers on time experience also make this distinction. Fraisse was perhaps the first in his *Les Structures Rythmiques* (Fraisse, 1956), along with Loehlin (1959) in his factor-analytic study. Michon (1967) states 'there is evidence that intervals of 3–5 s are evaluated by different processes than shorter durations'. Frankenhaeuser (1959) tested the effects of different procedures on both short and long time and found that some stimulant drugs affect short time but not long time.

Within short time, two separate processes may be distinguished. One is the immediate 'perception' or 'apprehension' of short intervals, the other the rhythmic-motor aspect of time, most properly termed *timing* as in Michon's (1967) study. The 'apprehension' of brief intervals is most often studied by presenting the observer with the interval and then obtaining his estimate of the length of that interval. Estimates of length may be obtained by asking the observer to reproduce that interval, or by obtaining a verbal estimation or other kind of estimation. Timing is usually studied using sequential stimuli and a key-tapping response. An important point to consider is that some variables which affect duration or one aspect of short time may or may not affect the others. Bell (1965) studied the effects of raising body temperature on time estimation using three separate measures. He found that the increase in body temperature increased the preferred rate of key-tapping and had no significant effects on counting numbers or on verbal time judgements. He concluded 'it may be that the rhythmic activity of time estimation methods has a greater susceptibility to changes in body temperature than the perceptual or intellectual aspects.'

The other continual mode of time experience is that of duration, our normal experience of time passing, of hours lengthening or shortening, of a recent event seeming 'a long time ago', of one interval passing more quickly for one person than another or more quickly for one person at one instance than another. It is the continuing, persevering, time in which we live our lives. Short time is continuing, but always fading from view, duration has some permanence. The experience of duration seems most keyed to remembrance of things past – to retrospection. So the experience of time may now be divided along the lines of memory – the present as short-term storage and the past, duration, as long-term storage. There will obviously be a high correlation between these experiences since they each involve memory, but not all that is in the short-term storage gets into long-term memory, so the correlation will not be perfect. There have been two major kinds of approaches to an analysis of these direct experiences of time – an approach based on the sensory process idea, and one more cognitive, based on information processing.

Before discussing these different approaches to continual time experience we should mention the other two major kinds of time experiences in order to obtain a clear view of the entire expanse of time experience and the limited range of any single analysis such as this.

The third mode of time experience is more socially determined than the other two. As with any other mode of experience the *direct* experience of time is subject to personal and social as well as intellectual interpretation. Different world views force varying interpretations of time experience.

Our general temporal perspective is derived from the kind of culture we live in. We in the West are very precise. We 'break' time up into small units; we can 'time' events very, very precisely. This concept is extremely useful in a complex, technological society. Our basic unit of time is the second as it has been for quite a while. We define it quite precisely as '. . . 9,192,631,770 cycles of the frequency associated with the transition between two energy levels of the isotope cesium 133' (Astin, 1968). Nakamura (1966) points out that other cultures, who are much less technically oriented than we, have different basic units of time (Nakamura, 1966). One Indian culture uses the time to boil rice as its 'basic unit' – how do you suppose that our technological culture could now get along with that sort of a basic unit? To study temporal perspective, other cultures are often studied to determine the distinctions between these differing time conceptions. Others have looked within our own culture for the time concepts of differing social classes (Le Shan, 1952) and these of differing philosophical orientations (Grunbaum, 1963).

The last dimension of time experience to be mentioned is that of simultaneity and succession. When do we experience events occurring at 'the same time'? What *is* 'the same time'? As Bergson pointed out, this depends upon the frame of reference, how fine the 'grain' of time experience (Bergson, 1965). If we take our second as the unit of time experience or $0 \cdot 1$ s as has been suggested by some (Stroud, 1956, 1967; White, 1963), we would obtain quite differing conception of what occurred at 'the same time' than if we considered all occurrences within the time to boil rice as 'at the same time'. This aspect of time experience has been discussed only by psychologically minded philosophers such as Bergson and has not, as yet, led to much empirical investigation save that stimulated by the idea of a 'perceptual moment' of $0 \cdot 1$ s in which all input information is processed, forming a potential neural substrate of the 'present' and of simultaneity (Stroud, 1956, 1967; White, 1963).

These are the four modes of time experience:

1. The present, short-term time.
   (a) The 'perception' of short intervals.
   (b) Rhythm or *timing*.
2. Duration, the past, long-term memory.
3. Temporal perspective – philosophical, social, cultural constructions of the world and their effects on the interpretation of time experience. 'Becoming', the future.
4. Simultaneity and succession.

This classification may aid in determining which data bear on each different mode of experience. It may help alleviate some of the confusion discussed by reviewers from Nichols to Adams since there might be contradictory processes postulated as 'time bases', but these may have been postulated to explain entirely different modes of experiences.

In the next chapter, we will discuss one of the ideas advanced as a building block of the continual experience of time – the 'time base'.

In searching for a suitable beginning point for an analysis of duration we must consider some approaches that bear on both short and long time, since many theorists have not made the distinction between them. There have been two major kinds of approaches to direct time experience – a sensory process idea – the 'time base' and a cognitive, information processing approach.

2 The 'Sensory Process' Metaphor

The number of biological or physiological theories advanced
to explain time experience has been characterized as a 'maze'
by more than one reviewer. Their similarity is this – all serious
theories postulate some sort of 'time base', a repetitive, cumulative, pulse-dispensing mechanism which delivers internal
time signals, an 'organ' of time. The 'time base' is identified
either with a specific periodicity which is then usually called a
'time quantum' or with a specific bodily process called the
'biological clock'.

Now let's review some of the evidence bearing on a 'time
base' analysis of the experience of duration. First we will look
at those approaches which identify the 'time base' with a
specific interval and use that interval as a sort of 'basic unit' of
time experience. These hypothesized intervals bunch around
either 0·7 s – the 'indifference interval' – or the 0·1-s 'perceptual
moment'. Secondly, we will look at some of the evidence and
theories which bear on the general idea of the 'internal' or
'biological' 'clock'. The purpose is to determine whether these
approaches relate *usefully* to the experience of *duration*, and if
not, to determine whether they are relevant to *other* modes of
time experience as a secondary consideration. This will hardly
be an exhaustive review, but major representatives of the
various approaches will be considered.

The 'indifference interval' arises out of one of the consistent
concerns of some time investigators – 'accuracy' with respect
to the clock. How well do we 'tell' time? At which interval are
we most 'accurate'? There is an obvious appeal in this
approach since it would simplify the analysis of time experience to the apprehension of an external process. This is the
sensory process idea, that there is a 'real' time existing

independently of ourselves which we 'perceive', 'accurately' or not. In ordinary speech we often assume this and call the clock 'real' time.

The typical 'accuracy' experiment is quite straightforward. By one of the time estimation methods, verbal estimation, reproduction or magnitude estimation, the observer is asked his judgement of the length of a presented interval. In any given experiment it is typically found that below a certain interval observers 'over-estimate' the interval compared to the clock. As the interval to be judged increases in length, observers tend to 'under-estimate' more (Fraisse, 1963; Woodrow, 1934, 1951). The interval at which the observer is 'correct' is the 'indifference interval'.

If time were a 'sense' then correspondences between experience and 'objective' time would be important. Some theorists, recent ones and those far in the past, have assumed that the 'indifference interval' must represent a kind of 'basic unit' of time experience since it is the point at which 'real' and experiential times coincide. As Woodrow states in his (1951) review; some have

... attempted to identify the indifference interval with the duration of some physiological event, such as the duration of the swing of the leg in walking or the time between two pulse beats. ... Others have attempted to connect the indifference interval with the duration of an alleged wave of attention, or, quite different, the time required to adjust the attention for the most effective apprehension of a stimulus.

One major problem with building a neural model of an 'internal clock' using indifference interval data is that one would then expect some consistency in the indifference interval if it reflected a basic neural process and that this does not seem to be the case.

Classically, the interval is reported to be 0·7 s (Fraisse, 1963). But it is in only a few of the many 'accuracy' studies that 0·7 s obtains as the result. The very first investigation by Horing reported the interval at 1·5 s. Since then, various investigators have reported different results, Kellert found

3·25 s as the interval (see Woodrow, 1934), Hulser at 1·8 s (see Woodrow, 1951), Treisman at 3·0 s (Treisman, 1963), and some have even reported two indifference intervals (see Woodrow, 1951).

As Woodrow (1934) summarized, these studies:

. . . show that there is no interval which can be said in the case of all subjects exactly to separate shorter uniformly overestimated from longer uniformly underestimated ones. They indicate that there can be no such thing as an indifference interval unless this interval be defined statistically in terms of some sort of average or most probable outcome.

In view of the large variability in the findings of these investigations one might more *profitably* view the indifference interval as arising from the particular stimulus and measurement conditions of each individual experiment and not as representing a basic physiological process within all observers.

But even if there were more coherence in the results of these indifference interval studies, Michon (1967) points out

. . . it remains less than evident, how processes which have intrinsic periodicities close to the indifference point could serve as a 'time base' unless we assume with Gooddy that they combine with all other periodic and quasi-periodic processes in the organism into a general 'clock form'. This view – also put forth by Carrel – may be philosophically valid, but it is hardly a suitable point of departure for a quantitative analysis of the time sense.

The idea that a certain interval is important for time experience merely because it is sometimes, under certain conditions, estimated 'accurately' seems to be fostered by the confusion of our arbitrary clock time of hours, minutes and seconds, with 'real' time. An attempt to find a 'time basis' for duration experience in the period of the indifference interval is based on the same kind of confusion of our clock with a 'real' time which led farmers in the American midwest recently to oppose daylight savings time because they felt that the extra hour of sunlight would burn the grass.

Others have looked to intervals shorter than that of 'indifference' for the 'time base'. White (1963) and Stroud

(1956, 1967) hypothesize that all input information during 0·1 s is integrated and processed as a runit. This is often called the 'perceptual moment' hypothesis. It has also been suggested by Norbert Wiener (1948) that the alpha rhythm of the EEG might provide the physiological mechanism underlying this 'time base' concept. The reason for this hypothesis is that the phase length of the alpha rhythm (8–12 c.p.s.) is very close to the 0·1 s of the 'perceptual moment'. In this view, the alpha waves are thought to act as the 'ticks' of a biological clock, these 'ticks' marking time and breaking succession from simultaneity.

To relate the brain's electrical activity in a quantitative way to time experience would provide a very solid empirical foundation for both the 'perceptual moment' and the 'biological clock'. However, there are some conceptual problems with this idea. Alpha is not always present in the EEG and there is no hypothesis as to what time experience would be during the absence of alpha. Does the 'clock' stop? Do the 'ticks' change rate when the modal frequency of the EEG changes out of the alpha range? But if this is so, when the modal frequency of the EEG changes, it is no longer close to the 0·1 s of the 'perceptual moment'. A less serious problem is that there seems to be no clear logic to the alpha-time hypothesis. The only reason alpha was implicated in this hypothesis is the coincidence of its phase length with the 0·1-s time of the 'perceptual moment'.

But an hypothesis does not have to be clear and logical to stimulate useful research. In this respect it is unfortunate that the studies which attempt to relate the EEG frequency to time experience have been uniformly unsuccessful. There have now been several studies on this relationship, those of Murphee (1954), Wright and Kennard (1957), Mundy-Castle and Sugarman (1960), and a quite extensive investigation in Legg's Ph.D thesis (1967), all of which have failed to show any quantitative relationship between the EEG and time experience.

It might be briefly mentioned here that the search for a quantum of *time* ought really be considered a search for a *neural processing* quantum. As Michon pointed out with respect to the indifference interval, it would certainly be unclear how a process with a periodicity of 0·1 s could serve as a 'time base' of *duration* experience since duration most obviously involves memory of the whole interval, that is, long-term memory. But if White and Stroud's view that all input information is processed in discrete quantized units of 0·1 s is valid, this might provide a 'time base' for the experience of *simultaneity*.

Instead of attempting to identify the 'time base' with a particular periodicity, others have sought to find a neurological, chemical or physiological process within the nervous system which might serve as the workings of an internal 'clock'. The alpha rhythm has already been mentioned in this context. As one would expect from the summaries of literature already quoted, there have been quite a few postulated 'biological clocks'. Among many, many others, Ochberg, Pollack and Meyer (1964) have investigated heart rate. Münsterberg (1899) suggested breathing rate, Hoagland (1933, 1935) brain cell metabolism, Bünning (1963) cellular metabolism, and Dimond (1964) and Braitenberg and Onesto (1960) other brain processes.

The concept of an 'internal clock' arises from the sensory process conception of time experience. The 'time base' in the indifference interval assumes an external time existing outside the organism, and the 'inner clock' is the hypothesized *organ* of time experience.

The idea relating a 'biological clock' to time experience is also derived from studies of lower organism's timing which often appears remarkably independent of the local environment. Since Garner and Allard discovered photoperiodism in plants there have been many attempts to cite longer rhythms, circadian or diurnal, or shorter biological rhythms (such as heart rate or alpha) as evidence for a 'biological clock'. Hamner (1966) points out:

Circadian rhythms have been found in such diverse phenomena as the loss of water by lemon cuttings, photaxis, such as the response to light of *Euglena*, the mating activities of *Paramecium*, and the size of the pigment cells in fiddler crabs.

We are naturally interested as to whether or not such rhythms exist in man. One immediately thinks of the sleep rhythm but it is difficult to prove whether or not this rhythm is truly endogenous. However, there are circadian rhythms in the blood eosinophil count, serum iron content, body temperature, heart rate, blood pressure, urine production and excretion of phosphate and potassium.

From these types of internal, periodic, processes and from the shorter biological rhythms, some theorists have tried to forge the link between our *experience* of time and these biological *times*. Often an attempt is made to modify the workings of a postulated 'internal clock' by physiological means such as the administration of a drug or by raising or lowering body temperature. Effects on time experience are correlated with the 'clock' manipulation.

As part of an extensive and fruitful series of studies, Fischer administered the drug psilocybin to his observers and studied the drug's effects on four processes as well as on the experience of duration. He noted that psilocybin lengthens duration experience, decreases the Weber fraction for taste, increases the size of handwriting, increases the chosen rate of finger-tapping and dramatically increases optical nystagmus. He concluded this way:

We have measured psychomimetric drug induced *chronostole* – time contraction – with the aid of four physiological chronometers, two sensory, one motor, and one psychomotor. These clocks evidently *do not run at the same rate*, i.e., central sympathetic stimulation does not result in the same rate of excitation for its various parts (Fischer, 1967).

Fischer's summary and conclusion brings to mind some of the problems of a 'biological clock' analysis of time experience. First, why are these four processes, the Weber fraction for taste, handwriting size, finger-tapping and optical nystagmus, termed 'chronometers'? What are the criteria for judging a given physiological process a '*chronometer*' – an internal time keeper? Why taste, as above, and not hair growth or heart rate or skin pigmentation? If one were to discover that toe-nail growth was speeded up or slowed down by psilocybin it presumably would be acceptable if one concluded that toe-nails were a 'chronometer'. If every physiological process is judged a 'chronometer' then what is the usefulness of the term? As we stated earlier, many other processes have been postulated as 'chronometers' – heart rate, breathing rate, cell metabolism, brain metabolism, alpha rhythm, etc. There are almost an infinity of physiological processes which might alter their rate in response to psilocybin or to some other manipulation, but this is not sufficient to term them a sort of internal time keeper, and to relate them to *time experience*.

The second problem is called to mind by Fischer's conclusion that the 'clocks' do not run at the same rate. There has never been any attempt to correlate any of the many processes which could be '*the* internal clock'. If *all* these various processes, heart rate, finger-tapping, etc., are 'chronometers' then which or what could be the 'biological clock'? Is it a combination of *all* these internal periodic rhythms, or just one, or some other combination?

We must conclude that, as we found an inability to determine any specific periodicity as a time base for duration experience, there is the same inability in linking this kind of 'time base' with any specific internal process. It would seem reasonable, in the case of Fischer's study to conclude, as he does, that psilocybin has differential effects on various peripheral processes, without assuming that these processes are in *themselves* 'chronometers' or internal organs of time experience. It is difficult for men to create new organs by assuming their existence. If we wish to relate Fischer's study to time experience, we might interpret his data somewhat differently and state that the changes in his four physiological or sensory – motor 'chronometers', taken together, are indicative of a central, cognitive state of increased sensitivity to external and internal stimuli. We might then conclude that it is more useful to assume that an increase in cognitive, information processing brought about by psilocybin lengthens duration experience rather than conceptualizing the drug's effects on an 'internal organ' of time.

A more consistent theory of the 'biological clock' was suggested by Hoagland (1935). His work began when his wife had a fever. Hoagland asked her to count at what she thought was the rate of one per second up to sixty. He recorded the duration of this 'subjective minute' and her oral temperature. He stated that the speed of counting and time judgements are temperature dependent. His conclusion was that these results on his wife 'indicate the existence of a master clock of a specific nature possibly the slowest in a series of irreversible processes involved in the respiration of certain parts of the brain' (Hoagland, 1933).

Hoagland then found that François (1927) had also studied the relationship between time estimates and body temperature. He then plotted François' and his own data as the log of the speed of counting against the reciprocal absolute temperature and found that the results approximated a straight line. He concluded that 'a unitary chemical mechanism is probably basically determining these judgements' (Hoagland, 1935).

In his general theoretical statement he states that the evidence on time experience is:

... entirely consistent with the hypothesis suggested in this paper of a specific chemical clock located in the nervous system and furnishing its possessor with a subjective time scale. Various changes in the immediate environment of this chemical clock may modify its velocity. Such changes may be those of temperature or of variations in the activity of sensory and motor areas of brain acting to accelerate or inhibit (experimentally primarily the former) the continuous chemical mechanism (Hoagland, 1935).

Hoagland's theorizing is quite impressive compared with his data which consist of very few observers run with extraordinary casualness, especially in view of the quantitative nature of his theory. He has not studied the problem further in the last 35 or so years except to reiterate his views in Fraser's collection of essays (Hoagland, 1966).

Others have attempted to study the effect of body temperature on time experience in the interim. Fox, Bradbury, Hampton and Legg (1967) performed two experiments and reported inconclusive results in one experiment and some time experience lengthening with increased temperature in the second. They state that marked individual variability found in their study and that of Bell (1965) and Kleber, Lhamon and Goldstone (1953), 'does not favour Hoagland's more specific suggestion that time judgement could depend upon one particular metabolic reaction in the brain.' Another experiment which provides some positive evidence for Hoagland's idea is that of Baddeley (1966) who lowered the temperature of his observers in cold water and found a shortening of time experience.

But the evidence for Hoagland's idea, on the whole, is mixed. Others have not confirmed his predictions. Bell and Provins (1963) attempted to repeat Hoagland's experimental paradigm. They artifically raised their observers' body temperature and found no significant differences in time experience between normal and raised body temperature. Bell (1965) raised his observers' body temperature by placing their legs in a hot water tub. He found that the 'speed of subjective time' increased in rhythm but not with any other measures. He concluded that Hoagland's suggestion that time judgements are determined by a chemical clock were not confirmed.

It would seem, then, on the basis of this evidence, that it is not very advantageous to consider a chemical 'clock' as a time basis. Hoagland's theory is not consistent with these data taken as a whole. It might be maintained, as do Fox, Bradbury, Hampton and Legg (1967), that the reasons for these inconsistencies between the theory and the data are due either to methodological inadequacy, as in Bell and Provins' study (1965) or to too weak manipulation of temperature, in Bell's study (1965). But the larger question is whether it is useful to consider time experience as temperature dependent or not. If one were to attempt an integrative theory of time experience based on a 'chemical clock' or on a 'biological clock' then one would have to interpret all the other 'clock' manipulations ultimately in terms of raising body temperature and also to interpret cognitive manipulations as raising body temperature a like amount. It would seem difficult to maintain that an increase in the number of stimuli which fill an interval (Fraisse, 1963), or an increase in 'perceptual motor load' (Michon, 1966), both of which lengthen time experience, will also raise body temperature. It would not be as difficult to maintain the reverse – just ask anyone who has had a fever. The argument is not that increases in body temperature (or the speeding up of a 'biological clock' with a drug) do not lengthen time experience, but rather that these manipulations are more parsimoniously considered as affecting cognitive processing rather than altering one of the maze of possible 'chronometers', heart rate, tapping rate, body temperature, cell metabolism, breath rate, etc.

To briefly summarize this review up to now. Although psychologists and physiologists and biologists have for a long period attempted to study time experience there has been a 'maze' of postulated possible mechanisms proposed for time. One major reason for this continuing scattering of effort has been that time has been treated as if it were a sensory process. If time were a sensory process like vision, then there would exist a 'real' time independent of us, and we would have an 'organ' of time experience such as the eye. Some have identified 'real' time with the clock time of minutes, seconds, etc.. They forget that our clock is but one arbitrary means of defining time. It is a convenience, used as an arbitrary standard, useful for meeting and making arrangements. But it is not 'real' time any more than the 'time' of boiling rice is 'real' or the cesium clock is 'real'. One may measure out one's life in coffee spoons as well as with a calendar, an hourglass or with pots of boiling rice. A 'time basis' of duration experience founded on the interval at which experiential and clock times sometimes coincide is of no special significance. Additionally, this interval is not even consistently estimated.

Another reason for the scattering of effort of time psychologists has been the lack of any over-all classification of time experience. One was attempted here, dividing time experience into four modes – short time, containing the 'perception' of brief intervals and rhythm; duration, a long-term memory based time experience; temporal perspective; and simultaneity.

In reviewing the 'biological' approaches to time experience, an attempt has been made to determine which evidence bears on each process.

A concept of a 'biological clock' may have some relevance in the explanation of periodic physiological rhythms *per se*, rhythms that come to a peak either around once a day or ones which are shorter. But these rhythms do not seem to provide any useful explanation of time *experience*. There seems to be no coherence in specifying an internal process which actually might be the 'clock'. Almost every process which might change rate in response to some environmental manipulation has been implicated, termed a 'chronometer'. But merely naming a given process a time 'keeper' does not usefully relate this process to time experience. These physiological rhythms might have some relevance for the tapping rhythm component of short time. Fischer found a consistent increase in tapping rate under psilocybin (Fischer, 1967), and of predictions from Hoagland's theory only rhythmic activity seems to follow consistently (Bell, 1965). Whether timing is most usefully conceptualized as based on an internal physiological 'clock' is doubtful. Michon (1966, 1967) shows alterations in rhythm speed related only to information processing. His term is 'perceptual motor load'. It would seem that a cognitive, short-term memory approach to timing (as Michon proposes) would be more parsimonious since the effects of drugs on the 'biological clock' might be interpreted as also increasing information processing. For the same reasons, a cognitive approach would seem more parsimonious for an analysis of the experience of duration.

The concept of a 'perceptual moment' of around 0·1 sec. in which all information is processed in quantal bits does not seem to aid an understanding of the experience of *duration*. The 'perceptual moment' might, however be usefully conceived as a 'time base' of the experience of *simultaneity*, on a molecular level.

What might be concluded on the basis of this review is that the old notion of an internal time 'keeper' rooted in a periodic biological process is not a *useful* concept for an analysis of *duration* experience, although various aspects of this 'time base' approach have relevance for other dimensions of time experience. In general, we have discussed two unfortunate confusions of many previous time analyses – the confusion of the experience of time either with the ordinary clock or with biological time.

3 The 'Storage Size' Metaphor

Since the 'time base' approach has proved not very useful for an analysis of the experience of duration, one might look to a purely cognitive approach as a theoretical guide. The rejection of a 'real' 'time base' has previously occurred in work in short time. Creelman (1962), using a signal detection model, ignores 'time base' and studies time perception in a wholly quantitative manner based on information processing. For the process of timing, Michon (1967) has prepared a carefully worked out information-processing short-term memory model and has performed a series of elegant experiments which confirm this type of model. In a roughly similar manner, duration also ought to be amenable to a cognitive, information-processing analysis which does not postulate any kind of 'time base'.

Before presenting the working hypothesis of this study some of the major cognitive ideas relevant to the experience of duration might be reviewed. There is the 'maze' of possible postulated cognitive influences on time experience as mentioned by Nichols but a prominent train of thought emphasizes some aspects of information processing. Guyau (1890) was perhaps the first theorist to relate time experience to human information processing. He felt that time *itself* did not exist in the universe, but rather that time was produced by the events which occur 'in time'. He thus considered time as a purely mental construction, from the events which take place. Time experience is constructed (he held) on the intensity of the stimuli, the extent of the differences between the stimuli, the number of stimuli, the attention paid to the stimuli, the associations of the stimuli and the expectations called up by the stimuli. Fraisse (1963) reviewed and summarized the many investigations on time experience and related time experience (both short and long) to the 'number of changes' which occur in a given interval. Frankenhaeuser (1959) performed a series of experiments which investigated the information-processing determinants of time experience and stated that the amount of 'mental content' in an interval determines its subjective duration. As stated earlier, Michon (1967) also emphasized information processing in his treatment of short time, in a much more quantitative and sophisticated way than had previous investigators.

If we are to approach the experience of duration as a cognitive process, we might consider a theory along the lines of Fraisse, Guyau and Frankenhaeuser. In all these cases, with more 'images' (the word Guyau actually uses), 'changes', or more 'mental content' the experience of duration is lengthened. This approach, then, would hold that the amount of information registered in consciousness would determine the duration experience of a particular interval. This would be a variety of short-term storage theory, an 'input register' which would monitor and measure the information input and be the basis for the experience of duration.

With this type of cognitive theory one might interpret the results of 'biological clock' studies very parsimoniously. The drugs which speed up a 'clock' also increase awareness of and sensitivity to the stimulus array. When more stimuli are 'registered' duration would lengthen. Such an approach would also account for the effect of increasing the number of stimuli in a given interval such as Frankenhaeuser (1959) who showed that with more 'beats' of a metronome, in an interval, time experience lengthens. Such an 'input register' type of theory could then integrate the two major trends in time analysis, the 'biological clock' and the cognitive approaches. It would additionally integrate short and long time experiences as dependent upon the contents of short term storage, as seen in Michon's theory of timing (Michon, 1967).

This type of purely cognitive theory almost perfectly accounts for the data of duration experience. There is only one area in which it does not hold. Duration is an experience which involves memory of the whole interval, an interval which is longer than the capacity of a short-term storage. The events in the 'register' must be stored somewhere and retrieved when the interval is over. This makes a purely short-term memory model less applicable to duration experience. Even though Frankenhaeuser was the first to draw an explicit link between duration experience and retention, her analysis in terms of 'mental content' does not fully account for the effects of memory on duration.

There is one body of data, in psychophysics, which illustrates this point. If observers are asked to judge durations of two successive stimuli, the first interval is often estimated shorter than the second. This is called the time-order 'error' (Woodworth and Schlosberg, 1954). 'Error' because the 'fading' of the first interval affects the 'accuracy' of the estimate of the second. Since we are not primarily interested in 'accuracy' with respect to the clock, these data might be viewed in another way. The estimate of the first interval shortens relative to the second. A theory based simply on the content of the 'input register' of each interval cannot account for these data since there would be no change possible of the short-term storage of an interval, yet the experience of the interval shortens. In order to account for these data we are forced to go back a little further into the system and to consider duration as a function of the information *remaining* in *storage* of a given interval rather than simply the information *input* during that interval. If the assumption be made that the information in storage of the first interval decays somewhat, then we can see that as this reduction in stored information occurs, time experience shortens. As Frankenhaeuser (1959) stated:

In respect of subjective time, . . . *succession is in itself an inherent characteristic of the experience.* Thus the discrepancy between the immediate perception and retention of time is not an error caused by methodological inadequacies which we want to eliminate, but rather a typical expression of the phenomenon we want to study.

This 'storage' approach is similar to the general 'input

register' approach except that the storage approach is explicitly a long-term memory theory and can account for the effects of time-order. Since there should be a constant ratio of decay of input information in storage across conditions, anything which increases the 'mental content' of a given interval relative to another interval will also increase the amount in storage of that interval relative to the other interval. Any of the effects of increasing input to the observer will then increase the amount in storage. This 'storage' approach also leads inquiry into other sources of influence on time experience, those which only influence the *memory* of a given interval and not the input.

We will adapt a cognitive, information-processing approach to duration experience, assuming that duration is constructed from the contents of storage. 'Constructed' is used in the sense of Bartlett's analysis of *Thinking* (Bartlett, 1958) or Neisser's *Cognitive Psychology* (Neisser, 1967). Time is even more amenable to a 'construction' approach than other cognitive processes such as the perception of contour since there is no physical continuum to be 'apprehended'.

The idea of a 'sense' of time may be useful in ordinary experience when one might want to compare experience to the clock – in cases when someone is habitually not 'on' time for instance, but as a scientific metaphor, the time 'sense' leads to a search for a non-existent organ of time experience and has not proven a useful guiding principle.

We replace the 'time sense' metaphor with a 'concept of time' similar to our concepts of order or of chaos, one formed out of the immediate data of experience. Duration may then be studied without reference to any sort of external clock, 'biological', 'chemical' or the ordinary mechanical clock. The experience of duration of a given interval may be meaningfully compared only with other experiences.

If duration is considered solely as a dimension of experience it is then unnecessary to determine whether this experience is 'accurate' or not with respect to the clock. Lumping time experience into two simple categories of 'accurate' and 'inaccurate' has seriously impeded the flow of work on time.

This type of categorization muddles differences between duration lengthening and shortening since both would be classified as 'inaccurate'.

The approach adopted here is a relational one with antecedents in the philosophy of relativity-oriented time analysts. Henri Bergson (1920) is the prime example, who assumed that time is properly discussed within each individual and that subjective time may speed up or slow down relative to other experiences within the individual or to other individual's experiences.

At this point the central metaphor of this paper will be more fully discussed. If we think of physical memories – to make our metaphor solid – we consider the computer. If information is input to a computer and instructions are given to store that information *in a certain way*, we can check the size of the array or the number of spaces or number of words necessary to store the input information. A more complex input would require a larger storage space than a simpler. An input composed of many varied items would similarly require more space than more homogeneous input.

If we think to human memory and time, we will try to relate the experience of duration of a given interval to the size of the storage space for that interval in general information-processing terms. In the storage of a given interval, either increasing the number of stored events or the complexity of those events will increase the size of storage, and as storage size increases the experience of duration lengthens. We now have a metaphor to guide research similar but more explicit than Frankenhaeuser's 'mental content' (Frankenhaeuser, 1959). This metaphor is not only somewhat less vague than hers but is also more explicitly a memory metaphor. If we wish to take the metaphor even demi-seriously there is one further point to make here. Just above, in introducing the computer analogy, I discussed information stored *in a certain way*. Not only is the actual information in storage important, but *how that information was stored* is just as important. The same amount of information or 'mental content' can, stored differently, subtend different storage sizes depending upon the way in which it was 'chunked' and laid down. Suppose you are asked to remember the following sequences of four binary digits:

1010   0100   1111   0111   1101

If you have no coding scheme for this sequence then this sequence would subtend twenty metaphorical spaces in storage. One space for each number in the input array. Suppose I give you a code. In this notation the zero always means zero and the ones, reading from right to left represent powers of 2. So the first (right hand) space if it is a 1 is 2^0 or 1, the next 2^1 or 2, the next 2^2 or 4 and the fourth in each sequence 2^3 or 8. So knowing the code you can store each four binary digit sequence this way – 10 4 15 7 13. Now the whole sequence subtends only 8 metaphorical spaces and the stored information is the same, since if you know the code you can produce 0100 from the 4 which is in storage. So the size of storage may depend not only upon the amount of information in storage but also on the way in which that information is coded.

Everyday examples of this abound. When trying to memorize a set of digits we try to induce a coding scheme. Ask anybody to remember the sequence 149217761968 read off quickly. He won't do too well. Then tell him that you are going to read off, in order, the year Columbus discovered America, the year the Declaration of Independence was signed, and this year. Then read the numbers off. Your friend will do better.

These coding 'tricks' apply at a higher level too. A woman at her first football game might look at an extremely complicated movement on the field which is coded by her male friend as a 'trap play', in the same way in the numerical example that someone knowing the code could store 4 while the inexperienced must store 0100. Men and women might reverse the efficiency of their coding mentioned above if they attended a dance concert.

The central metaphor of this paper, to replace a time 'sense' metaphor, is that the experience of duration of an interval is a construction formed from its storage size. This leads to a working hypothesis that anything which might alter the size of storage of the information in a given interval will also affect the experience of duration of that interval. As storage size increases, duration experience lengthens. Some procedures which might change storage size would be increasing or decreasing the input, or altering the coding or 'chunking' the input, or changing attentiveness to input or affecting the memory of the interval after the interval is over.

We are not then interested in how 'accurate' observers might be relative to the clock of hours, and minutes and seconds. The interest is in the *relative* duration experiences of different intervals. When observers are asked to judge duration they should be asked *directly* to judge the experience of one interval relative to another. For this purpose we will use a magnitude estimation scale, with the duration of one interval to be judged in relation to another interval, not to a clock time standard.

It would be useful now to review some of the 'maze' of the cognitive time perception data with the storage size metaphor in mind. We would expect that an increase in the number of events occurring within a given interval, or an increase in the complexity of these events, or a reduction in the efficiency in the way events are coded and stored, would each lengthen the experience of duration of that interval. We will try to determine how each separate procedure would affect storage size and then check the effect on duration experience to see if our approach does fit the data.

In all the approaches to time, either cognitive, or those of the 'biological clock', there is one general finding which seems most clear: when any procedure results in an increase in the number of stimuli perceived (and presumably stored) duration is lengthened.

One type of procedure is simply to increase the number of stimuli in the interval. Hall and Jastrow (1886) showed that an interval with many divisions (sounds) appears longer than one with fewer. In a very short sequence (perhaps within short-term time) Roelofs and Zeaman (1951) found that as the number of stimuli presented within that interval increased, time experience lengthened. Fraisse (1961) repeated and confirmed their results. Frankenhaeuser (1959) found duration lengthened with a metronome beating at 92 per min relative to it beating at 42 per min. Matsuda (1966) found that an increase in the number of 0·1-s 'clicks' from a rate of 0·5 per s to 6·7 per s lengthened duration.

If the reverse operation is attempted – a drastic reduction in external information – our metaphorical storage size should be reduced and duration experience should be shortened. One would therefore expect duration experience to be shortened in sensory deprivation. Banks and Cappon (1962) and Vernon and McGill (1963) have studied the experience of duration while in sensory deprivation. Both show duration experience shortening. In Vernon and McGill's study, thirty-three observers were studied for periods from 8–96 hr under sensory deprivation. The experimenters obtained duration estimates at the observer's release from the situation. The mean clock time of confinement was 54·25 hr, and the mean estimate of duration was 50 hr. Vernon and McGill concluded that time experience is shorter in sensory deprivation than normal. The problem with these results, and the conclusion of Vernon and McGill, although they would seem to follow quite nicely from the 'storage size' idea, is that one cannot state that duration experience *shortens* since there is no appropriate comparison. There are no data on these observer's estimates of long 'normal' intervals relative to the clock. The implicit assumption is made by these investigators that under 'normal' conditions 54·25 clock hours would be estimated 'accurately'. But we do not know this at all, under 'normal input' conditions 54·25 hr might be judged 30 or 60 hr. This is the difficulty of all studies which seek to relate the experience of duration to the clock. This difficulty is related to the old way of thinking about some 'absolute' or 'real' time existing independent of ourselves, to which our experience might be *directly* compared. Banks and Cappon's study does, however, include this sort of a control group. They had eight observers who underwent 'reduced input' conditions for 1·5 hr and also underwent a 1·25- or 1·5-hr 'control' interval. The 'control' condition was 'normal' input but they don't state exactly what the 'reduced input' condition was. Their observers gave clock-time estimates at the termination of each interval. They stated that the 'reduced input' interval was estimated less 'accurately' than the control interval. More importantly, all observers under-estimated the 'reduced input' interval more than they did the control interval. So the experience of duration is shortened with reduced input. Banks and Cappon's study might have been improved had they not been concerned with 'accuracy' related to the clock and had they asked their observers to estimate the duration of 'reduced input' directly relative to the 'control'.

There are other ways to change the information in the register without physically manipulating the actual stimulus array. The awareness of the observer may be changed so that he attends to more or to less of the stimulus array. This change has most easily been accomplished by the administration of an awareness-increasing drug. Normally the evidence from these drug studies is held to show the effect on the 'biological clock', as Fischer (1967) interpreted the results of psilocybin on time experience. Since it is clear that a 'biological clock' conception of duration experience is of limited utility we might view these data in another way. Since changes in input information affect duration experience it would be more parsimonious and integrative to assume that the effect of these drugs on the experience of duration is due to their effects on cognitive processing. From the storage size approach one would expect that drugs which increase awareness or alertness should result in more information from the stimulus array reaching consciousness. This should have the same result, then, as actually increasing the physical stimuli present – increasing the storage size of that interval and lengthening the experience of duration of that interval. Stimulant drugs should, then, lengthen duration experience and sedatives shorten it.

Goldstone, Boardman and Lhamon (1958) found that amphetamine lengthens duration experience relative to a placebo. Frankenhaeuser (1959) confirmed this, although administration of amphetamine lengthened duration relative to control, it was not statistically significant. The experience of duration under amphetamine was significantly longer than that under a sedative, pentobarbital. Frankenhaeuser also found that another stimulant, caffein, lengthens the experience of duration.

Probably the most striking alterations in awareness are obtained by the administration of the psychedelic drugs. These drugs, such as marijuana, psilocybin and LSD, produce a radical increase in the awareness of the observer. Fischer (1967) summarizes the physiological effects of these drugs, '[they] induce a central sympathetic excitation syndrome character-ized by . . . electroencephalographic activation . . . and of the synapses in the formatio reticularis which produce increased sensitivity to sensory stimulation.' Fischer himself presented confirmatory physiological data in his previously quoted study of the effects of psilocybin. Bradley and Elkes (1959) find EEG correlates of LSD showing desynchronization, indicative of cortical arousal. Purpura (1967) suggests the reticular activating system as a likely site of the action of LSD, linking it to 'brain stem reticular activation'. The RAS might be conceived as a kind of 'filter' of input and that under LSD or other psychedelic some of the normally closed 'gates' open.

Masters and Houston (1966), after fifteen years of research into the cognitive effects of LSD, confirm this 'opening-of-a-filter' phenomenologically. They state in their book, *The Varieties of Psychedelic Experience:*

. . . *for consciousness* a heightening of sense perception definitely occurs; but it may not occur in such a way as to be measurable by the tests now in use. We do doubt that the eye is absolutely seeing more, . . . or that the nose is smelling more. Rather, it seems likely that more of what the eye sees and more of what the nose smells is getting into consciousness. Some of this *more* doubtless results from the subject's paying greater and prolonged attention than he usually does but deinhibiting factors may be involved.

Fischer (1967) summarizes the phenomenological effects of the psychedelics in this way, 'there is (an) . . . amplification of sensing, knowing and attending' by the observer which he defines as bringing about a state of 'increased data content', or, as he quotes Gelpke (1967) 'a torrential flood of inner sensation'. Fischer (1966) also presents other physiological data such as increased speed of conduction of nervous impulses and increasing rates of cortical firing, both consistent with an increase in information processing. Key (1965) shows, in addition, an increase in the amplitude of the auditory evoked response (in a cat) under LSD. The lesser psychedelics have similar though not so striking cognitive effects as do LSD and psilocybin as seen in Bromberg's (1934) study of the effects of marijuana.

Reports of the effects of the psychedelic drugs on the experience of duration are unanimous – duration is lengthened relative to ordinary experience. All of Bromberg's observers experienced duration lengthening with marijuana, 'during the intoxication, time appears to be remarkably lengthened . . . The dense experience that crowds on the observer [makes] . . . what seemed like several days during it, was but a few hours' (Bromberg, 1934). Fischer quotes Delay *et al.* (1967) similarly on the effect of psilocybin, 'J'ai l'impression que le temps passe plus lentement, qu'il a plus de densité. Tout est d'une longeur indefinissable.' As reported earlier, Fischer (1967) also notes that duration experience is lengthened with the administration of psilocybin. Fischer, Griffin and Liss (1962), Ostfeld (1961) and Masters and Houston (1966), all report similar time-lengthening experiences with LSD. None of these studies include a control or placebo condition, a serious deficiency. This is somewhat mitigated by the fact that the observers in all these studies report lengthening of duration experience relative to their own ordinary experience and by the unanimity of these reports.

In reviewing these time experiences in these various situations, increasing the input by manipulations of the external stimuli or by the administration of an awareness-increasing drug, or decreasing the input by sensory deprivation, and the decrease in duration experience as the interval to be judged is farther away – all seem to follow a storage size interpretation.

When input is increased, the storage of that interval should be enlarged and duration experience lengthens. When the input is decreased, the storage size of that interval should be less and duration experience decreases. When some period elapses before an interval is to be judged (as in the time-order effect), some items should drop out of storage and the experience of duration of that interval shortens.

When these data are ordered with respect to 'accuracy' some important differences are muddled. Laurie (1967) for one, lumps LSD and sensory deprivation together as to their effects on time experience since each leads to 'inaccuracy' with respect to the clock. Again, the analysis is based on the idea that we are either 'correct' or 'incorrect' with respect to a 'real' time somewhere. If it is seen that this 'real' time concept is fruitless, then we are free to chart each effect on our experience, not relating it to the clock. In this case, the category of 'accuracy' obscures the fact that LSD leads to a lengthening of time experience, while sensory deprivation leads to just the opposite result.

We have settled then, on a cognitive metaphor for time experience, ruling out a physiological model based on a repetitive cumulative, pulse-dispensing, clock-like mechanism. But even if time experience is held to be cognitively determined, there must still be some brain structures which carry out the work. We want to relate time experience to the mechanism of attention, coding and storage in the brain rather than to a special internal organ of time experience. The brain structures underlying the storage size metaphor would need to be involved in the registration of input and its coding and parsing.

In several extensive and important series of experiments Pribram and his associates have begun to identify the brain structures involved in these processes. In his laboratory, Bagshaw (Bagshaw, Kimble and Pribram, 1965; Bagshaw and Pribram, 1968) showed that the autonomic components of the orienting reaction are no longer elicited after amygdalectomy. This brain operation also impairs habituation of the behavioural and EEG components of the orienting response, so Pribram (1969) reasoned that the autonomic components of orienting are necessary to the process of 'registering' the input; ordinarily the amygdala would act as a high order control over the servomechanisms involved in input regulation and thus one of the determinants of storage size – the amount in the register.

Pribram's second series of experiments is perhaps even more exciting. With Spinelli (Spinelli and Pribram, 1967) and with Dewson (Dewson, Noble and Pribram, 1966) he has investigated by electrophysiological techniques the control which the brain cortex exerts over input in the visual and auditory systems. In the visual mechanism, for instance, electrical stimulations of the 'association' cortex altered the size and shape of visual receptive fields recorded with microelectrodes from single units in the optic nerve and in the lateral geniculate nucleus of the visual pathway. Such results and many others like them suggest that the 'association' cortex of the brain does not really 'associate' anything. Rather, these cerebral areas, better therefore called 'intrinsic' (Pribram, 1969b), exert their influences on sensory input, organizing and coding it through subcortical connexions reaching all along the input pathways (Pribram, 1969b). Thus the intrinsic cortex, the so-called association areas of the brain, is vitally involved in the coding operations necessary to the cognitive metaphor of time experience.

Two lines of evidence give a clue to some of the specifics which might be involved in this coding operation. The first of these stems from one of the results of Pribram's input control experiments. It was found that the effect on input channels of intrinsic cortex stimulation was to change the amount of redundancy with which the input signal was processed. In fact, the posterior and frontal brain stimulations had opposite effects on the redundancy mechanism; posterior stimulations reduced and frontal stimulations enhanced redundancy.

The relationship between redundancy and time experience is well known. In reading a passage (or listening to one for that matter) the greater the redundancy, the faster the flow of the experience. Tight packing of information slows processing time. This relationship does not, of course, necessarily mean that the proper functioning of the posterior cortex slows while the proper functioning of the frontal cortex speeds time experience. But the experimental results do suggest such an hypothesis. Clinical neurological evidence can then be sought to support or disconfirm the hypothesis. Pribram and Melges (1968) have reviewed this evidence and, on the whole, the fit is not bad. The brain mechanisms serving the storage size metaphor of time experience are thus shown to determine not only the amount of input registered but also the amount of neural redundancy with which the input is processed.

The final line of evidence regarding brain mechanisms and the storage metaphor comes from yet another set of experiments delineating the functions of the frontal cortex. In these, a neurobehavioural analysis was performed of the impairment produced by frontal resection in monkey and man. Several series of experiments performed by Pribram and his collaborators indicated that the behavioural impairment produced by frontal lesions concerned the way in which input failed to be coded properly. Finally, an experiment was devised which showed the frontal impairment could be completely overcome if the task presented to the subject were properly parsed, i.e. given temporal stops which segmented the ordinarily continuous flow of input. The defect which follows frontal lesions can thus perhaps best be appreciated by us by recalling the old song, Marzydoats and Dozydoats (Mareseatoats) – completely meaningless until we realize that it refers to Mares and Does eating oats. Parsing, just as redundancy, affects 'storage size' intimately and is, of course, an important determinant of time experience.

The basic neural structure of a 'storage size' analysis seems to have been almost specifically investigated by Pribram and his associates. The amygdaloid complex has been shown to be involved in input registration; the 'association', i.e. the intrinsic, cortex with the modulation of redundancy and other simple aspects of coding such as parsing. All we would need further, if these suggested mechanisms are supported by further research, would be some storage mechanism which would store differentially as a function of the coding scheme.

That is too much to ask for right now.

The physiological upshot of the storage size metaphor is that a search for the neural correlates of time experience would not be for a special 'biological clock' system, but rather the mechanisms which underlie the registration and coding and storage of information.

Before becoming committed to the storage size metaphor, it should be tested in new situations to see its utility. The succeeding three chapters contain a series of experiments to explore the usefulness of the metaphor. Some of the specific questions studied are the effects of an increase in the stimulus input (assuming a corresponding increase in the input registered) on duration experience, those of alternate coding of the same stimulus situation, and some explorations into storage processes directly. These final experiments will attempt to test the storage size hypothesis more directly, to set it off more distinctly from the general kind of cognitive 'input register' type of theory. In these experiments, an attempt will be made to alter the contents of storage without manipulating the input at all, in the same way that the time-order effect shows that duration experience shortens with items dropping out of storage.

There are some common methodological points of these studies:

1. In all studies except the first, duration comparisons are made directly between the relative experiences of two intervals, not to the clock. This gives some more clear meaning to duration lengthening or shortening.

2. For the purposes of avoiding ordinary language confusions of time experiences (some people say that time is speeding up when we would say it shortens) all studies (except the first) use a magnitude estimation technique.

3. An effort will be made in all studies to keep the observers unaware that time is being studied. If they are aware that time is the dimension on which their judgements are to be made, we are less sure that our cues or coding schemes are actually used in the experiment. Observers who are aware as to the purpose of the experiment often assume it is some sort of 'test' and

attempt to be as 'accurate' or consistent as is possible and to count regularly to themselves or to tap their feet or to do something to nullify the whole experimental manipulation. In any case we are not really interested in how people estimate duration when they attempt to do so by counting, or by tapping, or in how well they are able to read their watches, but rather in their ordinary experience of duration.

4 Four Studies of the Stimulus Determinants of Duration Experience

If the experience of duration of an interval depends upon its storage size, then an increase in input to the observer should increase the input registered, increase the storage space of the contents of that interval and lengthen the experience of duration of that interval. This chapter explores three different ways of altering cognitive processing and the consequent effects on the experience of duration. The first experiment tests the effects of simply varying the number of occurrences in a given interval. This is to confirm the previous work of Frankenhaeuser (1959) and Matsuda (1966) and to clearly extend their findings to the experience of duration.

The second, third and fourth experiments are designed to explore qualitatively another dimension of stimulus input-time experience. We would expect that duration experience would be longer with increasingly complex input, even though the number of occurrences remain the same. This has not been demonstrated before, but would follow clearly from both the storage size metaphor and that of 'mental content'. As it should take more space to store an increase in events registered, it should take more space to store increasingly complex input.

The second experiment will test the effects of varying the complexity of a single visual stimulus on duration experience, somewhat like looking at different Mondrian paintings, graded for complexity. The third and fourth experiments explore the effects of varying the complexity of a series of stimuli – like musical notes – on time experience.

Experiment I

In this experiment, each observer listened to three tape

recordings, each of the same clock time length, 9 min and 20 s. On one tape in each series, events appeared at the rate of 40 per min, one at 80 per min, and one at 120 per min. There were two separate series of tapes, one with the stimuli appearing regularly and one with variable intervals between the appearance of the stimuli. The predicted result from the storage size hypothesis is that the 80 per min condition would be judged longer than the 40 per min condition and the 120 per min condition judged longest.

Method

Apparatus and stimuli. Two series of tapes were prepared, one with the stimuli spaced at regular intervals and one with the stimuli spaced by four different 'off intervals'. The stimuli were tones of 0·2 s, frequency 500 c.p.s. produced by an audio oscillator and played back through a Wollensak tape recorder to earphones. In addition, a Fels dermohmmeter and pen recorder were used as bogus brass instruments.

For each of the 'irregular interval' tapes four intervals were chosen to give average rates of stimulus presentation equal to that of the corresponding 'regular interval' tape. The 'off intervals' (those between the stimuli) for the 40-irregular condition were 0·74, 1·11, 1·49 and 1·86 s; for the 80-irregular condition, 0·27, 0·45, 0·64 and 0·83 s; and for the 120-irregular condition, 0·11, 0·24, 0·36 and 0·47 s.

The 'irregular interval' tapes were then constructed by consulting a table of random numbers for all numbers between 1 and 4 for as many intervals as would appear on the first $\frac{1}{4}$ of the tape. The interval sizes were then multiplied by 16 and these intervals along with a suitably modified tone were then put on tape manually by tripping one of four pre-set timers for each 'off interval'. The tape was then reduced by $\frac{16}{16}$ by the kind offices of the Memorex Corporation of Santa Clara, California. This completed $\frac{1}{4}$ of each tape. The stimulus order was reversed for each succeeding $\frac{1}{4}$ of the tape to avoid sampling problems. The actual number of stimuli on each tape were slightly different from the corresponding regular interval tapes but this was not thought to be a significant difference.

This difference is summarized below:

Table 1
Number of Stimuli on Each Tape (Experiment I)

	40/min	*80/min*	*120/min*
R	373	746	1119
I	368	737	1123

This same process was used for the regular interval tapes in order to equalize any frequency change error that might have accompanied the reduction process.

Observers. The observers were twenty-four Stanford University undergraduate students, eight female, sixteen male, recruited through a newspaper advertisement for an experiment on 'hearing'. They were told that the experiment paid $1·50 for 'less than an hour'. They were paid at the completion of the experiment.

Procedure. Os were run singly and assigned randomly to condition with the one constraint that the number of males and females be equal in both conditions. The order in which the tapes were heard was randomized. Os were told that they were to participate in an experiment investigating 'cognitive and physiological reactions to tones', and that 'this is an experiment which tests the relations between cognitive and physiological reactions'. They were told that the Fels dermohmmeter would measure their physiological reactions and that the questionnaire administered after each of the three tapes would measure their cognitive reactions. The instructions were concluded by E requesting O to remove all jewelry from his hands as the electrodes of the GSR were being attached. This was a convenient way to remove watches without making O aware of the purpose of the experiment. Each O listened to three tapes, all either the 'irregular' series or the 'regular' series. The questionnaire contained eleven items under the heading of 'tone quality'. The duration question was in the midst of these and was answered in terms of minutes on a line length scale of 1–20 min. A sample of the form of the questionnaire is reproduced in Table 2.

Results

The results from this experiment are summarized in Table 3. A 3×2 repeated measures analysis of variance was performed on these data (Winer, 1962) as shown in Table 4.

The results show that by increasing the number of stimuli within an interval duration experience lengthens. This lengthening is significant. There is no significant difference between the slightly different orderings of stimuli between the 'regular' and 'irregular' conditions. It was thought that these different orderings of stimuli might have some effect since the 'irregular' conditions were more complex than the 'regular' but the difference was too slight to be noticed by the observers.

Table 2

Questionnaire Items (Experiment I)

[···]

2. Pitch determination – were there any changes in the pitch of the tones in the series? ....
   If so, how many? ....

3. How pleasant was listening to the tapes?

---

5   4   3   2   1   0   —1   —2   —3   —4   —5
very   neutral   very
pleasant   unpleasant

[···]

5. How long was the interval that this tape was on?

---

1 min 2 3 4 5 6 7 8 9 10 11 12 13 14 15 16 17 18 19 20 min

[···]

7. How many tones did you hear? ....

[···]

9. How many different 'off intervals' were on this tape?..........

[···]

Table 3

Average Duration Estimate (in minutes) (Experiment I)

Stimulus rate	40/min	80/min	120/min
'regular' series	6·33	7·58	8·66
'irregular' series	6·50	8·40	9·33
Average	6·42	7·99	9·00

Table 4

Analysis of Variance (Experiment I)

	SS	df	Mean square	F	Sig.
Between subjects	274·94	23			
Regularity	5·55	1	5·55	0·45	ns
Subjects within groups	269·39	22	12·25		
Within subjects	133·34	48			
No. of stimuli	81·44	2	40·72	35·41	0·001
No. of stimuli × regularity	1·29	2	0·645	0·56	ns
Regularity × Ss within groups	50·60	44	1·15		

There were no differences between the conditions in reporting the variability of the 'off intervals'.

In this experiment the observers were asked to estimate their experiences of duration in minutes. This method introduces unnecessary variation in these estimates since each estimate must be translated into language related to the clock. It is of little interest to us how many minutes each observer rated each experience. Our concern is whether an increase in stimulus input lengthens duration experience *relative* to the other intervals, not to the clock. This result clearly does occur in this experiment, the 40 per min conditions are judged shorter than the 80 per min conditions, and both are judged shorter than the 120 per min conditions. If we present the results of this experiment as the group averages relative to one another, arbitrarily giving the 80 per min conditions the value of 1·00, we obtain:

Table 5

Results Expressed as Ratios of
Group Averages (Experiment I)

40/min	80/min	120/min
0·801	1·00	1·135

Even though the results obtained with a clock time estimate support the storage size hypothesis, in future studies observers will be asked *directly* to compare the duration of two intervals. A magnitude estimation technique would more directly tap the relative subjective experiences of two intervals as well as avoiding the complication of observers using different clock time words to refer to similar experiences. For instance, in this last study, one observer rated the 40 per min condition as 3 min long, the 80 per min condition as 4 min long, and the 120 per min condition as 5 min long, while another rated them 10, 11 and 14 min respectively. Since we are interested solely in the *relative* judged durations of these intervals, such differences in the way people are taught to label verbally their time experience merely tend to produce more variability in the results, without yielding any extra information. The magnitude estimation technique used will be described in the following study.

From the storage size hypothesis we can see that another determinant of the experience of duration might be the complexity of individual stimuli. As more space might be required to store additional events, more space would be necessary to store a more complex event. This suggests that the experience of duration should lengthen with increased complexity stimuli filling a given interval.

Experiment II

It is difficult to decide when one stimulus is more 'complex' than another. Several information theorists have addressed themselves to the problem of quantifying the complexity of line figures and have described procedures for generating figures of differential complexity. Attneave (1957) and Garner (1966) have described similar procedures. Attneave's technique, based on the number of interior angles of each figure was used here.

Method[1]

Apparatus and stimuli. Thirty-six stimuli were generated by Attneave's technique, four each with 4, 8, 12, 16, 20, 24, 28, 32 and 36 interior angles. For a validation of the generated figures' complexity thirty-five Os were asked to rate all thirty-six figures on complexity. The figures were split into two sets of eighteen each. When the Os completed rating the first set, they were given the second. In this way an average complexity rating for the thirty-six figures was obtained from 1–18. This rating correlated very highly with the theoretical analysis of the number of interior angles. These Os ratings were used as a basis for selecting the stimuli used in the experiment. Six were chosen, those which ranked closest to 2, 5, 8, 9½, 14 and 17 in the Os choice. Transparencies were made of the six figures. They are reproduced in Figure 1. The remainder of the apparatus consisted of a slide projector, the six slides and a screen.

Observers. The observers were 110 Stanford University undergraduates who participated in this experiment as a requirement for a psychology course. In addition, thirty-five other students served as judges for rating the complexity of the figures.

Procedure. When the observer entered the room, he was asked to sit in front of the screen (Os were run in groups of four or six). They were then told, 'You are about to look at

1. I would like to thank Mrs Leah Light for drawing the stimuli in this experiment and for help in running the observers and in data analysis.

two figures. We'd like you to look at them carefully as we are going to ask you some questions about them afterwards.' As the room was dark and duration was going to be compared *between* the two intervals, there was no attempt to remove *O*s' watches.

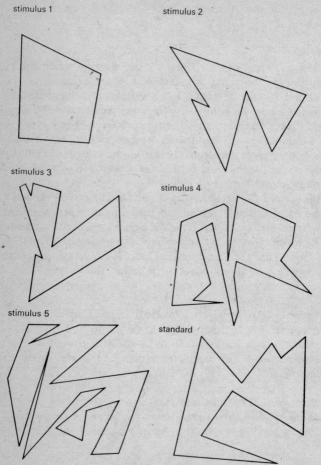

stimulus 1

stimulus 2

stimulus 3

stimulus 4

stimulus 5

standard

Figure 1   Stimuli used in Experiment II

The first figure shown to all Os was the drawing rated $9\frac{1}{2}$ on complexity by the judges. This was used as a 'standard' and was shown for 30 s. Os were assigned to one of five conditions, each group then viewing one of the other slides, also for 30 s. After viewing the second slide Os were given a magnitude estimation task. The instructions were:

On this sheet, given a line which represents the length of the first interval in which you looked at a figure, please indicate how long the second interval seemed to you, relative to the first. The length of the first interval is represented by the top line. If you felt that the second interval was longer than the first, mark off a line segment on the bottom line which is longer than the top line. If you felt that the second interval was shorter than the first, make the mark on the bottom line shorter than the top. If you felt they were about the same length, make the lines equal in length.

The scale is reproduced below.

First interval   ————————

Second interval ————————————————————

Results

The results are summarized in Table 6 in terms of the average ratio per observer per condition of the judged length of the second interval divided by the standard line length. If this ratio is above $1·00$ it would mean that the second interval was judged as longer than the first, if below $1·00$, the second judged shorter than the first.

Table 6

Results of Experiment II

Stimulus number	1	2	3	4	5
Duration ratio	0·81	0·92	0·99	0·96	0·965

Since the observers were run in groups of either four or six, the data were taken as group averages and treated as one observation. This gave an n of 5 for each condition and df of 9 for each t-ratio (see Table 7).

It seems that the increase in stimulus complexity lengthens

the experience of duration only up to a point and then further increases no longer have any effect. The increase in complexity from stimulus 1 to stimulus 2 leads to an increase in the experience of duration. Between stimuli 2 and 3 the increase is just not significant at the 0·05 level. Since the more complex stimuli give rise to the same duration experience, stimulus 2 was tested against all the more complex stimuli and was found to be judged significantly shorter than the average of stimuli 3, 4 and 5.

$$\left(t_2 - \tfrac{1}{3}(3+4+5) = 2\cdot319; \; t_{0\cdot05} \text{ (2-tailed) df } 19 = 2\cdot093.\right)$$

The results of this experiment seem to follow a 'channel capacity' of information processing. Many investigators have found that input information may be processed only up to a certain level of complexity, and above that level any excess information will not be processed (Miller, 1956). If the more complex stimuli were above 'channel capacity' then we would expect that the excess information would not be registered and the 'more complex' stimuli would be functionally the same.

Table 7

Summary of Statistics (Experiment II)

Comparison	t-ratio	Significance level (2-tailed df=9)
1–2	3·57	0·01
1–3	5·57	0·001
1–4	4·86	0·001
1–5	5·02	0·001
2–3	2·13	0·07
2–4	1·28	ns
2–5	1·42	ns
3–4	0·71	ns
3–5	0·57	ns
4–5	0·15	ns

A problem with the results of this experiment is that although they may be interpreted as showing that duration increases up to a hypothetical 'channel capacity' when the results from one stimulus are compared with one another.

There are additional difficulties with respect to the data from the comparisons of each stimulus to the standard stimulus. One should expect that stimuli which were less complex than the standard to be judged shorter, as was the case, but also that stimuli which were more complex than the standard to be judged longer. This was not found. If the 'channel capacity' interpretation is assumed then one could say that the 'more complex' stimuli were functionally equal to the standard and would be judged about equal to it. The data do show that stimuli 3, 4 and 5 were judged about equal to the standard.

Also surprising is the seeming lack of a 'time-order effect'. Given that the 'more complex' stimuli were functionally as complex as the standard, they were always presented second, and should have been judged somewhat *longer* than the standard. The ratios were all equal to or slightly less than 1·00, indicating no time-order effect. It is difficult to explain this finding on almost any theoretical approach.

This experiment may be interpreted provisionally as confirming a storage size analysis, with some difficulties. The interpretation would be that if the information in a stimulus can be processed, any increase in the input information will increase the storage size of that interval, duration lengthening with stimuli up to channel capacity. If an increase in the input information is above the processing capacity, then that increase will have no effect upon storage size and duration.

This interpretation needs some bolstering, either by more work on this particular study, varying the standard, the complexities of the stimuli, etc., or by other studies of stimulus complexity and duration experience. If these different studies support a storage size hypothesis then the results of experiment two can more securely be interpreted along storage size lines.

The number and complexity of individual stimuli seem to have effects on duration experience somewhat consistent with the storage size hypothesis. There is, however, more information in stimulus *sequences* than the sum of that in each individual stimulus. Any attempt to explain the experience of duration should also account for the way in which the entire *series* of individual stimuli are ordered – information displayed serially as well as all at once, as in music in distinction to viewing a painting.

Experiment III

Two situations may be imagined in which each contains the same number of identical physical stimuli, presented within the same amount of clock time. But there are possible effects of the *whole sequence itself* on storage size. It could be arranged so that one ordering of these stimuli allows more easy coding than does the other. Following the storage size hypothesis, it would be expected that the more easily coded experience would be judged shorter than the other.

Method[1]

Apparatus and stimuli. Two audio tapes were prepared, each lasting 5 min, each containing 200 sounds, at the rate of 40 per min or one sound every 1½s. Each tape contained ten different sounds repeated twenty times each. The ten different sounds were:[2]

1. Two hair brushes brushing together.
2. A quick three-note trill on a Kung alto recorder.
3. A typewriter key striking the roll.
4. A quick turn of the typewriter roller.
5. A quick wind of a stopwatch.
6. Zipping a zipper on a ski parka.
7. Tearing paper.
8. Blowing across a (Pilsner–Urquell) beer bottle.
9. Clinking of two Morinaga Milk Co. (Osaka) glasses.
10. A rubber band twanged.

For the 'easily codable' tape the sounds were distributed as follows: the first sound was played and repeated twenty times,

1. I would like to thank Mr Daniel Bernstein for making the tapes, running the observers and helping with the statistical analysis of this experiment.

2. I would like to thank the Department of Speech Pathology of Stanford University for the use of their sound-proof studio and tape-recording facilities.

then the second twenty times, and so on until all ten sounds had been played. For the 'random' tape the ten different sounds were played randomly at 1½-s intervals for 5 min. The order for these sounds was determined by the use of a table of random numbers. A random ordering of ten numbers twenty times each was transcribed and played by five people under the direction of Mr Bernstein.[1]

The remainder of the apparatus consisted of a tape recorder (Sony) driving four pair of earphones simultaneously.

Observers. The observers were twenty-four Stanford University female freshmen undergraduate students, naïve to the purpose of the experiment, recruited by Mr Bernstein for an 'experiment' which would last 'less than an hour' and were paid $1 each at the end of the experiment.

Procedure. Observers were run in groups of four. They arrived at the building in which the experiment took place and waited until all four were there. Mr Bernstein (who served as *E* for this experiment) then led the *O*s upstairs to the experimental rooms. As the *O*s entered the experimental rooms *E* asked them, 'I would like you to leave all jewelry, money and watches on the table during this experiment.' In response to questions it was indicated that this included keys, rings, necklaces, etc.

All then moved to the experimental room and were seated at a table in front of the pairs of earphones. *E* instructed them: 'I am going to play two tapes and I would like you to listen to them very carefully. Afterwards I shall ask you to answer a set of questions concerning what you hear. The tapes will follow each other with a brief pause in between them. Are there any questions? I'll be in the next room. Again, please listen carefully.'

E then left the room after turning on the tape recorder. He returned 20 s after the tapes were finished. He then said,

1. We all are indebted to Mr Bernstein for the precision of his description of the stimuli.

'Now please fill out this questionnaire about what you've just heard. The purpose is to find out what you've heard, so please answer as quickly as possible.' The duration question was similar to that of the previous study, being a magnitude estimation task, with the length of the 'standard' 50 mm and with the interval to be judged left open. In this case, however, there were two types of forms. One asked the length of the second interval to be judged relative to the first and the other asked the length of the first interval to be judged relative to the second. Each observer filled out one of these alternate forms. As there were also two orderings in which the tapes were played, there were four conditions.

Results

The results are summarized in Table 8 computed for the average ratio, per observer per condition of the judged duration of the 'random' tape interval divided by the length of the 'easily codable' tape. If this ratio was less than 1·00, the 'easily codable' tape would have been judged longer than the 'random'. If the ratio was greater than 1·00 the random would have been judged as longer. Note that, in the previous experiment, the different conditions were each compared to an experiential 'standard', and that in this experiment the two conditions are compared *directly* with one another. Since the observers were run in groups of four, all observations within each group were summed and treated as one observation, yielding an n in the t-tests of six.

Table 8

Results of Experiment III

	Questionnaire form		
	1st as	2nd as	average
Tape order	standard	standard	
'easily coded' played first	1·60	1·36	1·45
'random' played first	1·12	1·28	1·20
average	1·36	1·29	1·33 over-all mean ratio

The over-all result was that the 'random' interval was judged on the average to be 1·33 as long as the 'easily coded' interval ($t = 3·673$, $t_{0·02}$ (2-tailed) df 5 = 3·365). There was no significant effect on the judgements of the questionnaire form, while there was a time-order effect ($t = 2·168$, $t_{0·05}$ (1-tailed) df 5 = 2·015).

The experimental results in this study follow well from the storage size hypothesis. Even though the stimuli were of a very different order than those used in the previous studies, the increase in complexity increases the experience of duration. In order to further support the contention that the ordering of the stimuli, rather than the stimulus content itself, affects the experience of duration, it would seem that this study could be repeated using, again, an entirely different set of stimuli, visual ones displayed sequentially.

Experiment IV

The study of the effects of the arrangement of individual stimuli on the experience of duration was then repeated, this time using visual stimuli on slides.

Method

Apparatus and stimuli. The stimuli for this experiment were slides made of two Japanese line drawings, a Van Gogh painting, a Rousseau painting, a German expressionist poster, a close-up shot of marble, an out-of-focus shot of flowers, a photo of some pieces of pottery and two black-and-white line drawings. In short, these stimuli were intended to be very different from the ones used in the previous experiment and of a different order than the visual stimuli used in Experiment II since it is not the complexity of the individual stimuli which is being investigated here, but the complexity of the series itself independent of the content. The remainder of the apparatus consisted of a slide projector, slides and a screen.[1]

1. Again I am indebted to Dan Bernstein for helping to make the stimuli, for running the *O*s and helping with the data analysis.

Observers. Observers were twenty-four Stanford University undergraduates who participated in the experiment as a requirement of a psychology course.

Procedure. Observers were run in groups of four. The instructions and procedure were essentially the same as the last experiment with some important changes. First, the effects of the questionnaire form were not investigated, all *O*s judging the length of the second interval relative to the first. In addition, the time-order effect data were not taken, although the order of presentation of the stimulus series was varied, since, if the 'random' interval was always shown second, there would be a tendency to over-estimate the effect of the experimental manipulation. Last, and most importantly, the 'random' ordering was not the same as that in the previous study since a 200-unit slide projector was not available. Instead, fifty slides, five of each example, were pseudo-randomized and set in the carousel in positions 1–50. When this condition was run the slides were shown, at the rate of 1 per 1½ s from 1–50 and then the reverse order 50–1 was obtained by pressing the 'reverse' control on the carousel. The entire sequence was then repeated. The more 'easily codable' condition was also more easily run by the *E*. Slides were set in positions 61–70 and each was shown twenty times before moving to the next. Both intervals took 5 min, and, as in the previous study, 20 s elapsed between each condition. The instructions to the *O*s were the same as those in the previous study except for the obvious changes necessitated by the switch from auditory to visual stimuli.

Results

The results are computed in the same manner as above, the average ratio, per *O* of the judged duration of the 'random' series divided by the judged duration of the 'easily codable' series. This ratio was obtained by summing the total line lengths of all twenty-four *O*s for both conditions and dividing these. Taking a ratio for each *O* may bias the final obtained ratio.

Table 9

Results of Experiment IV

Average ratio $\dfrac{\text{'random'}}{\text{'easily coded'}}$ = 1·362

The more regular the stimulus input, the shorter the experience of duration. The obtained ratio is significant ($t = 3·86$, $t_{0·02}$ (2-tailed) df 5 = 3·365).

These last two studies show that the complexity of the *sequence* of stimuli, independent of the content of those sequences, affect the experience of duration. The more complex the sequence, the longer the experience of duration.

Experiments III and IV would lend themselves quite well to an alternate interpretation, one along the lines of 'habituation'. This would go as follows: in the 'easily coded' sequences what happens is that the repetition of the individual stimuli causes the observer to cease responding to input after the first few have gone by. When a change in the sequence occurs, O responds anew for a while and then ceases responding again. This does not occur in the 'random' conditions since they do not repeat themselves. Therefore the reason for the obtained differences in duration experience is that more stimuli are noticed in the 'random' conditions compared with the 'easily codable' ones.

This 'habituation' interpretation is certainly reasonable, and is also consistent with Experiments I and II. It is not a very different way of viewing these data, since if the results were due to habituation they would still be consistent with the storage size hypothesis, since the effects of habituation in this case would be to put differential amounts in storage corresponding to the duration estimates of the two sequences. The reason that these last two studies will continue to be interpreted in terms of coding and storage is that we have seen that a simple 'events noticed', or 'input register', theory cannot account for the effects of memory on time experience and additionally we will present some other experiments which affect coding and storage for which there is no 'habituation' interpretation.

We have now performed four studies of some stimulus determinants of the experience of duration. The effects of the number of stimuli, the complexity of a single stimulus and the complexity of a stimulus sequence were tested and, taken as a whole, they are consonant with a storage size interpretation. There is now a choice of the direction in which to proceed.

These four studies would lend themselves quite well to some parametric variations. It would be useful, in the case of the first experiment, to vary the number of stimuli more extensively to pin down the relations between number of input stimuli and duration experience. Is there an upper limit to input processing here as well as it seemed there was in Experiment II? Similarly, the second experiment lends itself to many kinds of variations which would more concretely base the 'storage' interpretation. The clock time of presentation could be varied, to bring this study more in line with the others, the complexity of the stimuli could be further investigated in order to delineate more precisely the hypothesized 'channel capacity' effect, as would some variations in the stimulus used as 'standard'. The last two studies perhaps lend themselves best to parametric variations and would provide a means of studying differences in input information and duration experience in a more quantitative way. One could vary the 'randomness' of the random tape so as to obtain several intermediate variability series and in this way plot a continuum of added information and relative duration experience. The four studies could also be performed in more similar situations, if one were to try and make a quantitative statement about these results. These would each be useful studies, which might lead to a more formal model of duration experience.

Such a model could be tested on the basis of these sort of studies. One could determine whether additional input linearly increases duration experience or whether the addition of new input has diminishing returns. One might determine whether the relative duration experiences of two intervals is determined by the ratio of their storage sizes or in some other way. Some more precise statement about the relationship of storage size to duration experience might be made in this way.

However, to perform these parametric type of studies and to build a model on these data would, at this point, be assuming what we are trying to prove. The purpose of this paper is not to build a precise model of the experience of duration, but rather to shift the emphasis of theories of duration experience from that of the hundreds of peripheral processes which might be a sort of internal 'clock', to a point a little further back in the system, a point at which the myriad of possible effects on duration experience might be integrated in terms of a central, cognitive, process. These beginning four studies clearly show that duration is usefully interpreted along cognitive, information-processing lines, since these studies replicate some of the cognitive effects of drugs which speed up an 'inner clock', and show the same effects on duration experience without speeding up any internal 'organ's' process. But although we have shown, on the basis of the time-order effect, and Frankenhaeuser's interpretation, that an analysis of the experience of duration must be a *storage* analysis, these four studies do not compel it.

The type of study which would most further our purpose would be some further *qualitative* investigations of the effects of some different orders of variation on the experience of duration. We would try and see whether the storage size hypothesis might make sense of duration experience in a variety of situations. These might include attention, coding schemes, and changes in storage size independent of the 'mental content' of the input.

The history of psychology and the present trends in psychology are filled with investigators attempting to attain the exalted status of *quantitativity* before fully exploring the questions before them. As Köhler pointed out some time ago, psychology is a young science, one whose problems are still in the process of definition not one whose problems are so clear that they are amenable to rigorous marching armies of quantifiers (Köhler, 1947). I would prefer to err on the side of generality and vagueness rather than prematurely decide upon a range of convenience of theoretical approach which would be precise and too limited.

The next chapter, then, contains two further investigations of the determinants of duration experience, experiments which explore the effects of attention, awareness and coding processes rather than those of stimulus array.

5 Two Studies of Coding Processes and Duration Experience

The previous chapter considered some of the stimulus determinants of the experience of duration. It was found that as the stimulus complexity increased the experience of duration lengthened. This was interpreted as consistent with the storage size hypothesis, since an increase in the number of stimuli or in the complexity of the stimuli should increase storage size.

If the experience of duration is determined by storage size, then factors other than the input should affect duration. One factor which might determine the experience of duration is the way in which the input is registered.

This chapter explores some structural variables which might affect duration experience – the coding processes by which input is selected, amplified or damped out. In short, we will investigate some of the determinants of the 'grain' of perception of a given situation and their subsequent effect on time experience. Manipulating the registration and coding of input, we would expect any construction which causes an increase in information processing to lengthen duration experience. In chapter 3, we mentioned that drugs which cause an increase in awareness of stimuli lengthen duration experience. In this chapter, two analogous sorts of situations will be studied in order to determine whether the effects of awareness on duration experience are consistent with the storage size hypothesis.

One way that the awareness of a given stimulus situation is changed is by its repetition. When we drive to work over the same route every day, we notice less and less of our surroundings as we continue driving over this same route. We 'automatically' respond to the stimulus situation. Even though it is clear that we are responding to the total stimulus situation (since we always arrive safely), when we perform a well-learned series of actions we are responding to the stimulus array in a different way than the first time we performed the action.

Saunders (1967) has performed a physiological experiment which bears on this. Using an avoidance conditioning paradigm he recorded the evoked response in the auditory cortex of a cat to the ringing of a bell. In the early stages of learning, each time the bell was rung, a large evoked response was recorded. The cat sometimes avoided the shock, sometimes not. When learning was perfect, 'automatic', each time the bell was rung the cat avoided the shock. But the cortical evoked response almost disappeared, showing that although the cat was obviously responding to the bell the sound was no longer getting into consciousness as it had before. For the present purposes, it can be seen that the 'automatic' state is one in which the stimuli and responses might be the same as on first presentation, but what enters consciousness on 'automatic' lessens.

This 'automatic' mode of awareness suggests an experiment related to duration experience. When the stimulus arrays and responses in two situations are similar, it would be expected from the storage size hypothesis that a person who could respond 'automatically' to the situation would be aware of less of the stimulus array and should then experience less duration than one who could not respond in the same way.

Experiment V

It would be useful to have a motor task to teach Os. Some would learn the task well, and some not at all. Those who are well-practised on the task should experience less duration during a similar period than those who are not familiar with the task.

Method

Apparatus and stimuli. The task chosen for this experiment was a pursuit rotor. This was selected because Os can learn to achieve a high level of proficiency within the normal time allotted to an experiment.

The apparatus for this experiment consisted of the pursuit rotor and stylus, a mirror-drawing console, and a tape recorder with a two minute segment of the 'random' tape of Experiment III.

Observers. The observers were thirty Stanford University summer students recruited by a paid recruiter and paid $1 for 'less than 45 min'. They were given no other information as to the nature of the experiment.

Procedure. Os were run individually and assigned to condition at random. There were three treatments of Os. All entered, and were told, 'This is an experiment which involves listening to a tape recording and also learning some task. Since you will be using your hands on an electrical apparatus please remove all jewelry on your hands including your bracelets, rings and watches.'

Os in the first condition then listened to the two minute segment of the 'random' tape. O was then explained the task of the pursuit rotor and worked at this task for 2 min. By means of a magnitude estimation relative duration scale similar to those of the preceding experiments O was then asked to compare his duration experiences of the 2 min working on the pursuit rotor to that of the 2 min listening to the tape. The 'tape' interval served as standard for all conditions in this experiment. This completed the experiment for Os in this treatment.

For the second condition, O entered, removed jewelry and practised on the rotor as follows: 2 min practice, 2 min rest, 3 min practice, 2 min rest, 2 min practice. These intervals were chosen because it was found that all pre-test Os learned the task very well in this interval. O then rested for 3 min and then listened to the 'random' tape, then worked for 2 min on the rotor and then answered the same duration question as did Os in the previous condition, comparing this last 2 min working on the rotor to the tape interval.

The third group was run in a similar manner to the second save that their practice was on an irrelevant motor task (mirror-drawing) for the four practice intervals. After the mirror drawing O listened to the tape and worked on the pursuit rotor for 2 min and then answered the duration question, comparing the 2 min working on the rotor to the tape. This condition was included to control for the possible effects of fatigue as an explanation for any differences between Os in groups 1 and 2.

Results

The results are summarized in Table 10, expressed as ratios for all the Os in a condition, of the line length drawn to represent the length of the work interval, divided by the standard line length (50 mm) representing the duration of the 'random' tape.

Table 10

Results of Experiment V

Condition	1	2	3
Ratio	1·56	1·09	1·42

t tests between the various pairs show that the 'automatic' condition is judged significantly shorter than the other two.

Table 11

Summary of Statistics for Experiment V

$t_{1-2} = 2·82$, $t_{0·02}$ (2-tailed) df 19 = 2·538
$t_{2-3} = 2·32$, $t_{0·05}$ (2-tailed) df 19 = 2·093

The no-practice condition and the irrelevant practice condition are not significantly different, $t_{1-3} = 0·58$.

These results are very clearly in line with the predictions. The well-practised interval was judged shorter than either an interval with no practice or one with irrelevant practice. While a task is being learned, as coding of the stimulus array progresses so that less of the stimulus array enters consciousness, duration experience shortens.

The results of this experiment also fall in line with those of Harton's experiment (Harton, 1939b) on the effects of 'success' and 'failure' on time experience. He found that successful experiences were estimated shorter than failure experiences. Harton interpreted his results as showing the effects of 'organization' on time experience. He felt that a 'successful' experience was more organized than a 'failure' and that more 'organized' experiences were estimated as shorter than disorganized ones. In storage size terms, a situation which was 'organized' would need less space in storage than a 'disorganized' one. Experiments three and four could be taken as confirmation of this, since 'organization' is redundancy.

The experience of being 'on automatic' is common but quite specific. It would be useful to investigate some more general types of coding processes. A recent major trend in perception has been in studying the effects of coding processes on which aspects of the stimulus array enter consciousness, on efferent modifications of input. Bruner, in a long series of experiments studies the effects of personality, expectation, familiarity, incongruity, etc. on perception. In his theoretical review 'on perceptual readiness' (Bruner, 1957), he discussed a mechanism in which as a function of 'set' or of these coding processes the brain could select out various portions of the input array and dampen out others. Pribram (1966) has been more explicitly concerned with the physiology of this efferent gating and modification of input, and has shown that information coming off the retina may be amplified or turned down by the brain. As Pribram says, 'the brain selects its input'.

There is more than just a passing similarity between analyses of selection of input at a neural or quasi-neural level and Kelly's (1955) theory of 'personal constructs'. Kelly applies the same type of analysis in terms of selection or modification of input to much more complicated stimulus situations. What 'objectively' occurs, for Kelly, is not as important as what is construed to occur.

There is some dispute as to how this process occurs. Neisser (1967) is more inclined to view this whole process in terms of 'construction' of experience rather than one of filtration and augmentation of input. For the purpose of time experience the specific process is not specifically relevant, although the general approach here smacks of both Neisser, in that time is held to be constructed form storage, and of Pribram, in that the mechanisms of input modification are implicated. Both sides. What is important for time experience is that almost all the recent work on perception has shown that the stimulus array is but one determinant of subjective experience and that with the same array, observers can have exceedingly different experiences.

It would be desirable then to investigate some of the general effects of coding processes on the experience of duration. But which aspects would affect duration? Most of the theorizing and work in this area has merely emphasized that different aspects of the situation may be perceived, or different experiences might be constructed out of the same situation. Merely changing the experience of a situation would not necessarily affect the experience of duration. We don't have any idea whether coding a situation as 'peaceful' or 'threatening' would have any effect on the experience of time. The sort of coding which might make a difference is the one analogous to the example given earlier of coding binary numbers into digital, reducing the storage space of a constant input.

In chess, for example, a novice might need to store the first ten individual moves of both players in order to remember the sequence. The master might just store 'Ruy Lopez opening' and be able to reproduce it with much less stored. These sorts of selection processes should also alter the experience of duration.

The next experiment will attempt to study the effect of coding schemes on duration experience. It would be necessary to have a constant stimulus situation, though complicated. This situation ought to be amenable to different coding schemes which would give different storage sizes. The best solution seems to use a film which could convey as complex a situation as necessary, yet be the same for all observers. Modern dance would be an ideal stimulus situation, since the number of movements are controllable yet abstract enough so that alternate codings of the same series of movements would be equally plausible to all (except modern dancers).

A way to extend the storage size hypothesis would be to teach different coding schemes by which differential complexity could be constructed out of the same stimulus array by different observers. Results consistent with the storage size approach would be that the more that is constructed to have occurred (given the same set of events), the larger the storage size and the longer the experience of duration of that interval.

Experiment VI

Method[1]

Apparatus and stimuli. A film was made of a dancer executing twenty-six modern dance movements in a series without stopping. The film was 1 min 40 s long. [2]

In addition, three training films were prepared from this 'dance' film. The first was prepared by splicing the dance into two segments, called the '2-element film'. These segments were of approximately equal length, each about $\frac{1}{2}$ the dance. The second, '6-element film' was prepared by splicing the dance into six approximately equal sections. The third training film contained the dance divided into eleven segments.

The remainder of the materials for this experiment consisted of a 16-mm film projector, a Sony tape recorder and the ubiquitous segment of the 'random' tape of Experiment III, this time 1 min 40 s long, to serve as a 'standard' for this experiment.

Observers. Forty-two Os participated in this experiment.

1. I would like to thank Mr Kareem Sadalla for his help in making and editing the film, and in running the experiment.

2. I would like to thank Miss Dorothea Ellsworth for performing as well as choreographing the dance sequence. I would also like to thank Mr Bob Moore of the Department of Communications, Stanford University, for essentially shooting the film for us, and Dr Henry Breitrose, also of the Communications Department, for allowing us the use of their studio and film-editing facilities.

They were all from an introductory psychology course and participated in the experiment to partially fulfil the course requirement. They were naïve as to the purpose of the experiment, and like all other Os in this study had never participated in a time experiment before.

Procedure. Os were run in groups of seven. There were three conditions, each containing fourteen Os. Each group was trained first, on one of the three training films. Each training film was shown twice during the training, Os learning to give a name to each segment. In the first condition, then, Os learned two elements in which to code the dance, in the second, six, in the third, eleven.

After training, each group listened to the tape which was to serve as standard.

The dance was then shown and the usual magnitude estimation task was administered, the duration of the tape as the standard a 50-mm line, the dance interval to be estimated relative to the tape interval.

Results

The results are expressed in terms of the average ratio, per observer, per condition, of the line length drawn to represent the length of the dance divided by the given length of the standard, the 'tape' interval.

Table 12

Results of Experiment VI

Number of constructs	2	6	11
Duration ratio	1·037	1·342	1·63

Since the Os were run in groups, the analysis of variance treated the data from each group as one data point, giving 6 data points and 5 df in the analysis of variance.

The differences over-all between treatments are as expected. A test for linearity shows that almost all the variability in these data are accounted for by the linear effect.

Table 13

Analysis of Variance for Experiment VI (Winer, 1962)

	SS	df	Mean square	F	Sig.
Between conditions	0·371	2	0·185	23·13	0·025
linear contrast	0·350	1	0·350	43·75	0·01
residual	0·021	1	0·021	2·62	ns
error	0·024	3	0·008		
Total	0·395	5			

The results of this experiment show that, given a stimulus array, when more is construed to have occurred in that array, the experience of duration lengthens. This effect is quite similar, in some ways, to the effects of the awareness-increasing drugs discussed in chapter 3. Comparing a person who has been given one of these drugs to a normal person shows that the one who is on the drug experiences a speeding-up of cognitive processing and also a lengthening of duration experience. In a similar way this experiment compared the effects of increasing the amount which was construed to have occurred out of a given array, and found the same order of results.

In the two studies in this chapter, it has been seen that when stimulus conditions are equivalent, the way in which the stimulus array is coded may have effects on the experience of duration consistent with the storage size hypothesis. In the first study the coding which arises out of familiarity with the situation was studied. This last study investigated a more general kind of coding procedure, the effects of the category or construct system on the experience of duration.

The results of these studies follow from the storage size hypothesis. We found earlier that an increase in stimulus input (in a variety of ways) lengthens duration experience. In these last two experiments, the differential coding of input affected duration experience in the same ways as had the previous four studies. When more of the stimulus array was registered, when more was construed to have occurred, the effects on duration experience were the same as those of physically increasing the input information. The important variable, then, is the input which is registered and stored, not merely that in the stimulus array. An increase in the input registered and stored increases the storage size of that interval and lengthens the experience of duration of that interval.

These first six studies make a cognitive, information-processing approach to the experience of duration necessary. They replicate the cognitive effects of the 'biological clock' studies without speeding up an 'inner clock'. These first six studies show that by directly increasing cognitive processing the experience of duration is lengthened. Since the drugs which speed up an 'inner clock' also speed up cognitive processing and lengthen duration experience, it would seem more parsimonious to state that the determinant of that experience is in cognitive processing. If not, one would have to say that, in the first case, an 'inner clock' is being speeded up, and in the second that cognitive processing determines duration experience. But, as we saw earlier, it is quite difficult to maintain an 'inner clock' type of explanation since there has not been any agreement on what could be the 'clock', or how a 'clock' such as heart rate, body temperature, etc. could give rise to time experience. In addition to these problems, it now becomes unparsimonious to maintain this type of explanation.

If a cognitive, information-processing approach to duration experience is necessary to account for these six studies and the data reviewed earlier, it is also clear that these six studies in themselves do not compel a *storage size* type of cognitive explanation. In order to demonstrate that a storage size approach is necessary, we must point to some evidence which shows that the storage size of an interval might change without changing the input registered or the 'mental content'. If duration experience changes along with the storage of an interval then we may conclude that a storage size type of cognitive, information-processing approach is necessary, rather than the 'input register' type.

6 Three Studies of Storage Size

The last two chapters have explored some of the possible effects of some procedures which alter input information, processing of that information and the coding of that information on duration experience. We found these effects to be consistent with a storage size interpretation. The storage size metaphor, though, leads inquiry into other areas.

We have looked so far at the effects within a given interval upon the stimulus information reaching awareness (and thus storage) and have found them to be interpretable along the lines of the storage size analysis. But up until this point there is no theoretical line of demarcation from the other variants of cognitive approaches. An 'input register' type of theory could account for all the data presented so far in this paper. The data from the first six experiments compel a cognitive, information-processing approach but not necessarily a *storage* type.

If the experience of duration depends upon the contents of storage indexed to a given interval, then it should be possible to modify the experience of duration by altering the contents of storage by measures taken *after* the input is registered. In discussing the storage size metaphor in chapter 3, I stated that the *size* of the storage space depends not only on the content of storage, but also on the way in which the information was stored. In Experiment VI by learning a more comprehensive code the size of storage of a given amount of information might be reduced. If similar procedures could be used successfully on information in storage, then we could alter storage size without altering any of the 'mental content' of the input of that interval. It could then be shown, without changing anything which occurred during the interval *itself*, that when more is in storage of that interval, or when the contents of storage of that interval are less efficiently 'chunked', that the experience of duration lengthens.

One body of relevant data has already been mentioned, that of the time-order effect. Before going on to an experiment which explicitly attempts to recode the storage of a given interval, it would be useful to repeat and refine the time-order effect, since we have made it the critical piece of data on which we rejected an 'input register' type of theory. Conditions could be arranged so that some observers would retain more about a given interval than others. This would allow some comparison between two groups of observers, instead of one, as in the time-order effect. It also would be useful to determine whether there is *actually* a difference in the amount in storage between these two groups, instead of making the assumption that this is the case, as we did in discussing the time-order effect.

Experiment VII

For checking the amount remaining in storage it was thought ideal to use a learning task. After some pretesting it was found that words paired with certain 'harsh' sounds would be forgotten more quickly than words paired with 'neutral' sounds. Since this pairing did not affect learning time, at the completion of the learning task there would be no difference in the number of words remembered. At some later time, there would be a difference in the number of words remembered of that interval with no further manipulation on our part.

The predicted results from the storage size hypothesis are as follows: immediately following the interval, when there will be equal amounts in storage of the 'harsh' and 'neutral' conditions, the duration experiences of the two groups should be equal. Later, when the observers in the 'harsh' sounds condition have forgotten more than those in the other group, duration should be judged shorter in this condition than in the other. The duration estimates of all four groups should then co-vary with the amount in storage.

Method

Apparatus and stimuli. Two tapes were prepared, each containing ten words paired with ten sounds, for a paired-associate learning task. The tapes were played on a Sony tape recorder through earphones.

Observers. The observers were forty-eight Stanford University undergraduates, twelve in each of the four conditions. They were told that they would be paid $1·50 for an experiment lasting 'less than an hour'.

Procedure. Observers were run individually and assigned at random to condition. When *O* entered the room, he was asked to remove any jewelry, sat down in a chair and instructed to listen to a tape. 'I would like you to listen carefully to this recording as I am going to ask you some questions about it later.' This tape was to serve as a standard and was a 5-min segment of J. S. Bach's *Musical Offering*. When the tape was completed some instructions followed.

When you hear a bell ring, a learning task will be begun. This task consists of some sounds paired with some words. Your job is to learn which sound goes with which word. After the first time the series is finished, each time a sound appears please say the word which follows it, even if you have to guess. You will then hear the correct word and will know if you are correct or not. Keep doing this until the tape ends and a final bell sounds.

Every *O* learned the list in the seven trials. The seven learning trials took 6 min. When the second bell rang, demarcating the interval to be judged for *O*, *E* turned over a card which told him whether *O* was to give his duration judgement then or in 2 weeks. The time judgement was the same as those in the previous experiments, a magnitude estimation comparison of the learning interval with the interval filled with the music.

If *O* was to give his judgement then, he did so, was paid, asked not to discuss the experiment with friends and left. If *O* was to give his duration estimate at a later time, he was simply paid the $1·50, also asked not to discuss the experiment and sent home. O was given no indication that he was to be called back. This was done in order to avoid, as much as possible, Os practising on the task. These Os were called 12 days later and were asked to come in on a day which was two weeks from the original test date. They were told that they would be paid an additional 75 cents for 'less than 15 min'. All Os returned. When these Os returned they were immediately given the duration question and then retention was tested by playing the learning tape and recording the number of correct responses on the first trial. This served as the operational measure or the amount in storage.

Results

The results are expressed in the usual ratio of the length of the line drawn to represent the duration of the learning interval divided by the 'standard' line length (50 mm) of the music interval.

Table 14

Results of Experiment VII

| | | Point When Duration Estimate Was Taken | | | |
		Immediately		Two weeks later	
			0·26		
	neutral	1·21		0·95	1·08
Stimuli during training					
			0·52		
	harsh	1·29		0·77	1·03
		1·25		0·86	

The relearning test data were:
Number correct on first trial
'harsh'   4·8
'neutral'   7·3

There is an over-all effect of the two week delay on the experience of duration of the test period. The estimates taken later were significantly shorter than those taken immediately, $t = 2 \cdot 879$, $t_{0 \cdot 01}$ (2-tailed) df 47 $= 2 \cdot 704$.

There is no over-all effect of the 'neutral' and 'harsh' stimulus conditions, $t = 0 \cdot 364$.

There is a significant difference within the results two weeks later. The duration estimates of the observers in the 'harsh' condition is significantly lower than that of those in the 'neutral' condition, $t = 2 \cdot 213$, $t_{0 \cdot 05}$ df 23 (2-tailed) $= 2 \cdot 069$.

A test of the differences in the reduction of duration estimates between the 'harsh' and 'neutral' conditions, testing $0 \cdot 52$ against $0 \cdot 26$, over the two weeks is significant, and in the expected direction, but only by a 1 tailed test, $t = 1 \cdot 865$, $t_{0 \cdot 05}$ df 23 $= 1 \cdot 714$.

The number of words identified correctly on the first re-learning trial were significantly larger in the 'neutral' condition, $t = 4 \cdot 68$, $t_{0 \cdot 001}$ (2-tailed) df 23 $= 3 \cdot 767$.

Immediately following the interval, when retention was equivalent in both conditions (all observers had perfect scores on the last learning trial), duration experiences were equal ($1 \cdot 29$ is not different from $1 \cdot 21$, $t = 0 \cdot 347$). But two weeks later, when more was retained in the 'neutral' condition, than in the 'harsh', that condition was judged longer than the other.

Without changing anything which occurred during the interval, without altering anything which could affect information-processing or an 'input register' during that interval, over a period of two weeks, items drop out of storage and, as they do, the experience of duration decreases. This experiment, coupled with the data from the time-order effect, yield a more clear 'storage' interpretation of duration experience than do any previous studies.

Now that the time-order effect is confirmed and given a little added weight by including a measure of the amount in storage, we might return to considering the effects of the organization of the storage on the experience of duration, how the information is stored.

There have been two mentions of the relationship between organization and time experience. Loehlin (1959) performed a factor-analytic study of time estimation, his data obtained by questionnaire. His main finding was that the more an interval constitutes a 'unit' in the observer's experience, the shorter was the experience of duration. Harton (1939a) also proposed that organization affects duration experience. He gave his observers either many tasks to perform in a given interval or just one. (The total number of movements were equated.) Those who had just one task to do judged duration as less than those who had many tasks to do. Harton interpreted these results to show that the more organized the task, the shorter the experience of duration. Several of the experiments in this study have been interpreted in this manner. In informational terms, a more 'organized' stimulus is one with more redundancy, less information. Coding binary numbers, in the example in chapter 3, made them more 'organized'.

In Experiment II there seemed to be an increase in duration experience with additional information up to a point. In Experiments III and IV, the more organized interval, the more 'easily coded' interval was judged shorter than the more complex interval. Similarly, in Experiment VI, when the dance was 'better organized' in the observer's experience, when it was coded into fewer categories, his duration experience decreased.

It takes less space to store something which is redundant, i.e. a 'unit' as opposed to a more complex, less organized experience. If we could code an experience into a 'unit', we should decrease its storage size and shorten the experience of duration. This next experiment is an attempt to directly alter storage size by coding an unorganized experience into a unit *after* the interval is over. We stated earlier that storage size depends primarily on two factors: the amount of information which reaches awareness of the observer and the way in which that information is coded and stored. We saw in chapter 3 that the same amount of information could subsume different storage sizes if it was coded differently.

Therefore, if storage size is a determinant of the experience of duration it might then be possible to alter that experience by actively manipulating the storage of an interval *after* it is over. This was done in a way in the previous experiment, and the time-order effect might be taken as evidence for this but it would be most useful to manipulate more directly the contents of storage by providing a means of recoding what is already in storage, reducing the size of storage by a new procedure.

Experiment VIII

One way to do this would be to use a figure similar to the Gestalt (Koffka, 1935) figures which could be coded in either a simple or complex manner, by instructions. We could have observers view the figure given a complex set, and then, after the interval is over recode it more simply for them and see whether this recoding reduces their experience of duration. Another condition could be included, in which the simpler coding be done before viewing the figure. A control condition would have to be included in which observers view the figure give a complex set and given no further coding. Comparing the simple coding before the interval with the complex would in essence repeat Experiments VI and II. The advantage of using a line drawing is that the recoding may also be done *after* the interval. If recoding after the interval alters duration experience then the results in all the previous studies will more clearly and parsimoniously be considered as storage size effects and not simply as a function of an 'input register'. If this type of recoding after an interval can change duration experience then this, coupled with the time-order effect and the results of Experiment VII would provide strong support for a storage size interpretation of duration experience. In this experiment we would like, again, a measure of the amount in storage in all conditions.

Method

Apparatus and stimuli. The 'test stimulus' for this experiment is reproduced in Figure 2, the 'complex set' stimulus in Figure 3, the 'coded set' stimulus in Figure 4. The stimuli were reproduced on ditto paper in the experiment.

The remainder of the apparatus for this experiment consisted of a tape recorder containing a 1-min segment of the 'random' tape of Experiment III.

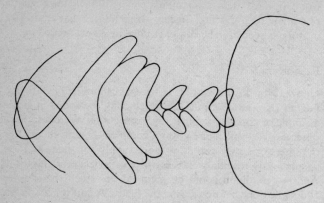

Figure 2 Test figure for Experiment VIII

Figure 3 'Complex set' figure for Experiment VIII

Figure 4 'Coded set' figure for Experiment VIII

Observers. Forty-eight observers participated in this experiment, all students in the introductory psychology course, receiving one credit for their participation in this experiment. They were given no information as to the nature of the experiment. *O*s were run in groups of twelve, four in each of the three conditions simultaneously.

Procedure. The first figure examined by all groups was one of the 'set' figures. These instructions were read to all *O*s.

'This experiment involves looking at some line drawings and listening to a tape recording. Please pay careful attention as comparisons will be asked of these drawings and sounds. Please turn over your books. The first drawing is an example of the kind of figure you will be looking at.' Twenty seconds elapsed. 'Now close your eyes and carefully listen to this tape.' The tape played was a 1-min segment of the same 'random' tape which has been used in several of the preceding experiments. After the tape was played, *O*s were instructed to open

Table 15

Schematic Plan of the Procedure of Experiment VIII

	20 s view	1 min listen	1 min view	20 s	Duration est.
1	complex set	standard tape	test stimulus	wait	tape/test int.
2	coded set	standard tape	test stimulus	wait	same
3	complex set	standard tape	test stimulus	view coded set figure	same

their eyes and to turn over the next page in their booklet, on which was the test stimulus. After viewing this for 1 min, *O*s turned over to the next page. In the case of the first two conditions, the page was blank. For the third condition, this page consisted of the 'coded set' stimulus with these words written on it: 'What you have just seen was the word "man" written over its mirror image.' After 20 s had elapsed *O*s were instructed to turn to the next page and answer the duration question. This question asked them to compare the length of the tape with that of the interval following the tape.

After answering the duration question, *O*s then were asked to write a description of the test figure, as if they were 'describing it to a friend'. This was done firstly as a check on whether the coding manipulations had any effect. They did – only one *O* in group 1 for instance, used the word 'man' in his written description. More importantly, the number of words used to describe the figure were taken as a measure of the size of storage of that interval.

Results

The results of this experiment are shown in Table 16. The analysis of variance is summarized in Table 17.

The over-all differences between groups are significant. Comparison 1 shows that coding, either before or after the interval, makes a significant reduction in duration length. The individual comparisons on the effect of coding before the interval and after the interval (3 and 4) each show significant

Table 16

Results of Experiment VIII

	Duration ratio	Number of words used to describe 'test stimulus'
1	0·98	64
2	0·68	22
3	0·76	31

Table 17

Analysis of Variance for Experiment VIII (Winer, 1962)

As the Os were run in groups of twelve at a time, four in each condition, all those run at the same time in the same condition were treated as one observation reducing the n in this analysis from 48 to 12.

Source	SS	df	Mean square	F	Sig.
Between condition	466·45	2	233·22	12·94	0·005
comparison 1	425·04	1	425·04	23·58	0·001
comparison 2	41·40	1	41·40	2·29	ns
Error	162·26	9	18·02		
Total	628·71	11			

If we break up the between conditions SS another way to get a direct test of the reduction of duration from groups 1 and 3:

comparison 3	214·24	1	214·24	11·88	0·01
(residual)	252·21	1	252·21	13·99	0·005

Similarly, we might divide the between conditions SS so as to get a direct test of the differences between groups 1 and 2:

comparison 4	433·48	1	443·88	24·63	0·001
(residual)	22·57	1	22·57	1·30	ns

Table 18

Coefficients of Comparisons in Analysis of Variance for Experiment VIII

Group	1	2	3
Orthogonal comparisons			
1	+2	−1	−1
2	0	+1	−1
Non-orthogonal comparisons			
3	+1	0	−1
4	+1	−1	0

reductions in duration experience. Finally, whether the interval is coded before or after seems to make little difference – comparison 2 is not significant.

These data provide the most compelling confirmation of the storage size hypothesis. Up until the point of recoding, there can be no difference expected between Os in groups 1 and 3 since they received *exactly* the same treatment. Therefore the experience of duration can be reduced *after* an interval is completed by changing (recoding) the storage of that interval. That the storage is changed may be seen in the data from the number of words used to describe the test stimulus, which are reduced from 64 to 31 ($p > 0.001$) by the coding manipulation.

The differences between groups 1 and 2 (comparison 4), tend to confirm and integrate the findings of two earlier studies. This procedure is similar to that of Experiment II in that with increasing stimulus complexity, duration experience was lengthened, only in this case the increase in complexity was accomplished by coding processes and not in the stimuli themselves. This comparison also brings it together with the sixth experiment which also tested the effects of alternate coding schemes on the same events. A storage interpretation can account for all these findings, while a simple metaphor of 'mental content' cannot.

Since the last experiment provides the most unambiguous evidence for the storage approach, and makes the other experiments more clearly and consonantly interpreted along these theoretical lines it would be useful to confirm and extend the findings of this last experiment. A replication would be useful as would at least another degree of complexity of coding at which the restructuring of the interval and its relation to time experiment could be tested. This is more easily desired than accomplished, since it is highly preferable that *all* the information in the stimulus array be codable in various ways, and be codable *post hoc*.

After searching in vain for another stimulus which could be codable in three ways I returned to the stimulus used in the previous study. When you first looked at the 'test figure' you might have thought it was a complicated insect. It was designed with that coding possibility in mind. In fact, five of the eighteen observers in the previous experiment's 'complex coding' condition (1) mentioned the word 'insect' in their written description. These observers also reported shorter duration experience than did the remaining thirteen in this group. Even though the 'insect' code was mentioned by some observers it was thought that giving an 'insect' set to all observers in a condition would reduce the average storage size of that interval somewhat, although not nearly so much as the 'man' coding. This would provide two more data points relevant to coding one before, and one after the interval.

Experiment IX

Method

Apparatus and stimuli. The 'insect set' stimulus is reproduced in Figure 5.

The other stimuli and apparatus were the same as those of the previous experiment. For the 'recoded insect' condition, the 'insect set' stimulus was used along with the written words, 'What you have just seen was a drawing of an insect, with its head to the left and tail to the right.'

Observers. Sixty Stanford University undergraduate students served as observers on this experiment. They were recruited and paid $1 for 'less than $\frac{1}{2}$ hr'. They were given no information as to the nature of the experiment.

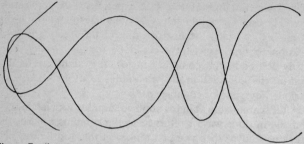

Figure 5   'Insect set' figure for Experiment IX

Procedure. The procedure was exactly the same as that of the previous study save that *O*s were run in twelve groups of five each, one *O* per condition per group. *O*s were assigned randomly to condition.

Results

The ratio, per *O* per condition of the test interval/music interval is summarized in Table 19:

Table 19

Results of Experiment IX

	Duration ratio	*No. of words*
1 No coding before or after	1·097	73
2 Coded insect before interval	0·873	37
3 Coded insect after interval	0·921	49
4 Coded 'man' before interval	0·681	26
5 Coded 'man' after interval	0·783	38

The analysis of variance of these data are summarized in Table 20. This analysis was made using the ratio of the line length divided by the standard length, while in the previous study the analysis of variance was done of the untransformed data – this does not alter anything save the absolute magnitude of the sums of squares and not the F-ratios.

Table 20

Analysis of Variance for Experiment IX (Winer, 1962)

Source	SS		df	Mean square	F	Sig.
Os in groups	0·366		11			
Between conditions	1·185		4	0·296	11·65	0·001
comparison 1		0·784	1	0·784	31·36	0·001
comparison 2		0·333	1	0·333	13·11	0·001
comparison 3		0·057	1	0·057	2·24	ns
residual		0·008	1	0·008	<1	ns
Error	1·119		44	0·0254		
Total	2·670		59			

As in the previous experiment, we can divide the between conditions SS in alternative ways so as to test other hypotheses. Comparison 4 tests the effects of coding after the interval:

	SS	df	Mean square	F	Sig.
comparison 4	0·505	1	0·505	19·88	0·001
residual	0·680	3	0·227	8·94	0·001

Comparison 5 tests the effects of coding before the interval:

comparison 5	0·821	1	0·821	32·32	0·001
residual	0·364	3	0·121	4·76	0·01

Table 21

Coefficients for Comparisons for Analysis of Variance for Experiment IX

Group	1	2	3	4	5
Comparison 1	+4	—1	—1	—1	—1
2	0	+1	+1	—1	—1
3	0	+1	—1	+1	—1
4	+2	0	—1	0	—1
5	+2	—1	0	—1	0

There is an over-all difference between conditions. More importantly, comparison 1 shows that the complex coded condition was judged significantly longer than all the more simply coded ones. Comparison 2 shows that the two conditions coded as 'insects' were estimated significantly longer than the 'man' codes. These conditions are each intermediate between the 'man' coding and the complex coding. This difference goes along with significant differences between the number of words used to describe both the insect figures and both the 'man' figures ($t = 4.86$ $t_{0.001}$ df 40 = 3.55), and between the two 'insect' figures and the uncoded figure ($t = 4.48$, $t_{0.001}$ df 30 = 3.646). Comparison 3 shows that there is, again, no significant difference between coding before and coding after the interval.

The two non-orthogonal comparisons (4 and 5) show that there are significant reductions in length of duration by coding *after* the interval (4) and coding *before* the interval (5).

The results of this experiment both directly replicate those of the previous experiment and provide a somewhat stronger indication of the effects of storage size on duration experience. If a stimulus is decoded into two different levels of complexity, both before and after the interval, the experience of duration will decrease as the stored complexity decreases.

In this chapter the storage size analysis has been extended into new areas. This approach has led inquiry into new kinds of influence on the experience of duration, those events which occur after the interval is completed. This kind of effect follows from the storage size hypothesis and is very difficult to encompass under any other type of theoretical analysis of duration experience. A 'time base' or 'internal clock' idea does not contain a possibility of a *shortening* of the experience of duration with new input, since these models all assume some variety of a repetitive, cumulative, time-building process. In a similar way, the cognitive 'input register' type of theory might adequately account for the results of Experiments I through VI, but cannot account for the memory effects on the experience of duration, the time-order effect, the effects of items differentially falling out of storage as in Experiment VII, and the restructuring of the information in storage by recoding after the interval in these last two experiments. The storage size hypothesis can make sense of the 'biological clock' effects on time experience, the cognitive manipulations of increasing input to the observer, coding the stimuli so that different amounts of the stimulus array reach the observer, and the effects of events *after* the interval. It then seems the most *useful* way to consider the experience of duration.

7 Summary, Conclusion and Some Speculation on Future Directions

We began by posing a question which has probably occurred to many reflective persons at least once in their lives – 'What, then, is Time?' We immediately found, as is so often the case in science, that there is no simple answer to this question, because 'time' is not one, nor five, nor ten things, but more. Several of the many 'times' were mentioned, the time of the poet, the philosopher, the physicist, the psychologist, the biologist, the times of the sundial, the calendar, the time to boil rice, the time of the hourglass. Time is each and all these and more.

We were concerned more with the times of the psychologist, the times of experience, especially that of *duration*. In reviewing the literature of time psychology, there seemed to have been a great confusion as to how time experience arose within ourselves. As Nichols (1891) said:

It has been declared *a priori*, innate, intuitive, empirical, mechanical. It has been deduced from within and without, from heaven and from earth and from several things difficult to imagine as of either.

One reason for this confusion might have been a lack of demarcation of the variety of the times of experience. Since these have rarely been explicated some may have had an insight as to the nature of one mode of experiential time and then proposed it as the basis of time experience in general. In vision we would not confuse determinants of the hue of an object with determinants of its form, so in the analysis of time experience we ought not confuse, say, simultaneity with rhythm. In general, an appropriate method for a scientific analysis is to attempt to determine *under which conditions* a given theory applies, instead of assuming that any given approach can account for very different experiences. For this reason, I listed four modes of time experience and made an attempt to determine the relevance of time theories to these modes of experience. These dimensions of time experience were marked off:

1. Short time
    (a) Rhythm
    (b) 'Immediate apprehension' of brief intervals
2. Duration
3. Temporal perspective
4. Simultaneity and succession

In linking particular theoretical approaches with modes of time experience we found that the other major reason for the confusion in time experience was that time had been considered as if it were a sensory process such as hearing. This type of analysis would presuppose external time stimuli, existing independenlty of ourselves as do sound waves, which would be apprehended by an *organ* of sensation, like the ear. Many have looked for such a 'time base' in an internal organ of time experience.

The 'time base' has been identified either with a particular periodicity or with a particular physiological, neurological or chemical process, termed a 'clock' or 'chronometer'.

The periodic 'time bases' centre around two intervals. First, the 0·7 second 'indifference interval' which is said to be the point at which 'real' time is 'accurately' apprehended. If this could possibly be true, then there might be some consistency in the results of these 'accuracy' studies. This is not the case as the indifference interval has been shown to vary by at least an order of magnitude. One cannot assume that 'real' time is varying that much and that these results reflect this. Rather one could best consider this interval as an artifact of the particular stimulus and measurement conditions of a particular experiment and having little or nothing to contribute to an understanding of our experience of time. The supposed importance of this interval stems from the confusion of the experience of time with a 'real' time – the clock. This sensory process conception of time experience has led to this kind of confusion. This has always been a problem. There was great consternation long ago when the millenium approached, some fearing the end of the world merely due to the date.

The other interval postulated as a 'time base' is that of the 'perceptual moment' of 0·1 s. White (1963) and Stroud (1956, 1967) have assumed that all input information during this interval is integrated and processed as a unit. It can be seen that if a concept of serial, discrete, information processing is valid, that this might serve as a 'time base' for the experience of *simultaneity*.

The attempt to identify an *organ* of time experience has resulted in the postulation of an 'inner clock', identified with a particular process. This conception is bolstered by the fact that many of the physiological processes in the body show periodic rhythms, such as the circadian rhythms of the blood, body temperature, etc. (Hamner, 1966) and the shorter rhythms of breath rate, heart rate, etc. The essential question is whether these rhythms are related to our time *experience*, and whether it is *useful* to relate them. Certainly when the 'biological clock' is speeded up by the administration of a drug, duration experience lengthens, as in Fischer's study of psilocybin (Fischer, 1967). But what could be the 'clock'? Almost everything possible has been considered as the 'clock' or 'chronometer', the heart, the cerebellum, pacemakers in the brain, the respiration cycle, the Weber fraction for taste, cellular metabolic rate, etc. If *all* these could be *the* 'clock' then the concept of the 'clock' could have no meaning. There is no consistent identification of the 'clock' in any one of these processes, and no real way that an 'inner clock' would relate to time experiences.

If the other line, the cognitive approach, to time is considered, we find that one particular relationship has been found: when an attempt is made to increase the amount of information processing in a given interval, the experience of that interval lengthens. Several theorists have proposed theories of time experience based on these data. All assume an 'input register' which measures the amount of 'mental content' of the interval and, from this, time experience is constructed.

A cognitive, information-processing approach would be more integrative and parsimonious than a sensory process conception. The effects of the drugs which speed up the 'biological clock' also increase information processing and therefore, both situations can be accounted for by the cognitive type of theory, where the 'biological clock' either must state that, say, heart rate increases when the stimulus array is more complex, or that duration experience is determined by *both* an 'inner clock' and cognitive processing. The first assumption would have no evidence at all to support it, and in fact, no one has proposed this. The second assumption merely preserves the unclarity of the 'inner clock' concept and makes it even more cumbersome. The cognitive approach seems a much more useful way to consider these data.

There is but one problem with the 'input register' theory. Frankenhaeuser (1959) pointed out that duration experience involves long-term memory and contrasted immediate time 'perception' with retention, although her theory did not take this into account. Duration must involve a memory of the entire interval, longer than the fleeting 'input register' storage. The time-order effect shows that any approach to duration experience must be a storage one, not merely an 'input register' type. These theories are of similar order, the only difference being that the 'input register' holds that duration experience depends on the *input* information during the interval, while a storage approach holds the information *remaining in storage* determines duration experience. These two approaches, obviously, predict the same result in most situations, since the information input and that stored are highly correlated. It is only in effects on duration after the interval that there is distinction. The storage approach can deal with the time-order effect as well as all the data which is consistent with an input register.

The metaphor chosen to account for the experience of duration was a storage one. We said that duration depends on the size of the storage space for the information of a given interval. The size of the storage space would depend on two factors: the amount of information or number of occurrences in the interval which reach awareness and the way in which that information was 'chunked' and stored. The same amount of information might subtend different storage sizes depending on how efficiently it was coded.

A cognitive approach need not study the relationships between 'objective' time and experiential time as would a sensory process conception of time experience. The duration experience of a given interval need be compared only to other experiences, and not to any other kind of clock, one of hours and minutes, or one of biology, or one of quantum mechanics or one of mathematics.

The nine studies presented here represented a progression. Beginning with the most general effects, the central idea was extended to include coding processes and finally a clear demonstration of the storage determinants of duration.

The first experiment showed that an increase in the number of stimuli filling a given interval lengthened duration experience. The second experiment showed somewhat equivocally that, as the complexity of a stimulus increased up to a point, duration experience lengthened, and that further increases above that point no longer increased duration experience. The third and fourth studies confirmed the tentative result of the second. In these, the stimulus complexity also was increased and duration experience lengthened, but the increase in complexity was accomplished by varying the whole sequence of stimuli, rather than the individual stimuli as in Experiment II. Even though they are not the most standard, parametric type of experiment, they correlate the experience of duration to information theory in a more precise way than had previous investigators, providing a more clear definition of 'mental content'. These studies also deal with much longer intervals than had previous investigations. The first four studies would be interpreted as follows. It takes more space to store new events, so that an increase in the number of events in an interval should increase storage size and lengthen the experience of duration of that interval. It also takes more space to store increasingly complex events (in the information theory sense) so the experience of duration should lengthen as the complexity of the stimuli or of the *sequence* of stimuli increase. In the second study, this was the case up to a point, and then the increase levelled off. This was interpreted to be a point at which no further information could be processed, no further increase in storage size could be expected, and no further lengthening of duration experience should result.

The information in the *stimulus array* had, by all investigators, been considered the sole cognitive determinant of duration experience. What has been overlooked are the ways the information is coded or selected. We know from modern research on perception that there is an efferent involvement in perception, a means by which we can select out aspects of the stimulus array and dump out others. Information in the stimulus array will not affect duration experience if it is not registered.

The two experiments in chapter 5 attempt to study coding processes. Experiment V showed that when an observer is in a position to 'automatically' respond to a stimulus array he experiences less duration than one who cannot respond in the same way. This was interpreted as confirming the storage size analysis, for Saunders (1967) has shown that when a cat responds 'automatically' to a stimulus situation, he is less aware of the stimuli around him than while he was learning. If less enters consciousness 'on automatic' then less would be in storage of that interval and duration experience should shorten. It is a common experience among truckdrivers, who drive over the same route often, to find themselves far along the route, with no recollection of having driven there and having experienced no or little duration during that period. Repeating a familiar action is very likely to result in this 'automatic' mode of responding to stimuli.

Experiment VI studied the general effects of coding a stimulus array. The stimulus situation was much more complex and 'social' than were the previous experiments. It was found that, when a stimulus situation is efficiently coded chunked into few elements), the experience of duration shortens. Since we stated that storage size depends not only on the information input but additionally upon how that information is selected and coded, these two studies confirm and extend the storage size hypothesis.

The first set of experiments was a confirmation and extension of previous cognitive, information-processing approaches to duration experience. They provided a more solid base of evidence for a cognitive interpretation. The second set of experiments extend the 'mental content' or 'input register' type of theory to include the structural variables controlling the way in which the input is selected, coded, and stored. Although the storage size metaphor is a little more specific and relates in a slightly more quantitative way to information theory than does the 'mental content' type of theory, the evidence so far in these six experiments does not compel a *storage* approach, but a general cognitive one.

The last three studies attempt to demonstrate that the crucial determinant of duration experience is the size of storage of the interval, not necessarily the input registered. In order to show this, we would need to alter the size of storage of an interval *without changing the input*. Experiment VII attempted to demonstrate more clearly that the time-order effect is due to items dropping out of storage, consequently duration experience shortening. When conditions were arranged so that observers in one condition forgot more than observers in another, the experiences of duration co-varied with the amount in storage. The group who retained less of the information in an interval estimated that interval as shorter even though, when that interval was just completed, the duration estimates were equal. This more clearly shows the storage size effects on duration experience than had previous studies. This experiment also sheds some light on why 'pleasant' or interesting experiences are likely to be regarded as 'long' in retrospect when they were not in passing. The reason is that these experiences are apt to be better retained than ordinary experiences and then, compared to them at some later date, will seem to have been very 'long'.

If duration experience depends on the size of storage of the information in a given interval as seems indicated by the previous study and the evidence of time-order effect, then it should be possible to alter the experience of duration of an interval by altering the way in which the information in that interval was coded and stored. If this manipulation could be done *after* the interval was over, then there could be no explanation for any effect on duration experience other than the altered storage size.

The final two studies in this paper accomplished this effect. By recoding a 'random' or complex stimulus into a simpler one after the interval was completed, the experience of duration was shortened relative to those who did not recode the stimulus. In Experiment IX, it was shown further that this encoding could take place at two levels of complexity. A stimulus might be coded fairly simply or less simply and the duration experiences co-varied with the complexity of the coding. The 'insect' set took more words to describe and was judged longer than the 'man' set, but this insect set took fewer words to describe and was judged shorter than an uncoded set.

Two other conditions were also included in Experiment IX, coding *before* the stimulus was viewed. The same order of results was found, the 'insect' judged shorter than uncoded and longer than the 'man'. These conditions repeat the results of Experiment II and show that stimulus complexity (*as coded*) affects duration experience in a way consistent with the storage size hypothesis. These two conditions also repeat the general paradigm of Experiment VI, in that coding schemes allowed differential complexity to be coded out of the same stimulus array. In both cases, when more complexity was construed to occur, the experience of duration lengthens. These two conditions tend to buttress the results of Experiment II, and integrate it with Experiments III, IV, VI, VIII and IX. These studies could all be interpreted as showing that when stimulus complexity *in storage* increases, either by physically increasing the complexity or by coding the stimuli in a more complex way, duration experience lengthens. The remainder of the studies (I, V and VII) could be interpreted as showing that when the *number* of stimuli in storage increases, duration experience lengthens.

This last series of experiments yields the most direct evidence yet for a storage size interpretation of the experience of duration. When no manipulations are attempted during the interval to be judged, nothing which could alter the 'mental content' of the input information, duration experience varies with the way that the information is coded and stored.

Conclusion

Returning to the beginning question, 'What is time?', we have gone through all this to find that we cannot answer it. Time is too diverse a concept to be amenable to one answer. Time is many things, many processes, many types of experience. We cannot even answer the much simpler question, 'What is the experience of time?' – since we have seen that time experience is not a unitary 'sense'. The different times of experience will require different types of explanation. A theory which might account for the experience of simultaneity might not handle the experience of duration.

Instead of proposing an approach to encompass all of time experience, I have tried to determine the relevance of various approaches to different areas of time experience. I have tried to determine under which conditions each type of approach might apply.

We cannot judge an approach on whether it is 'true' or not. Every theory is 'true' to some extent. The criteria on which a theory might be judged relative to others are those primarily of utility. Can one interpret a larger amount of relevant data under one approach than another? Can this be done parsimoniously? Does the approach serve as a useful guide to further inquiry?

On these grounds, considering duration experience to be determined by storage size seems the most useful approach. The storage approach alone can integrate the diverse data of duration experience. These data include: the lengthening of duration under LSD or the other psychedelics, the effects of a 'successful' or a 'failure' experience, those of sensory deprivation, the number of stimuli present, 'unity of organization', the complexity of stimuli, the time-order effect, the administration of a sedative drug or of a stimulant drug such as amphetamine, the way a stimulus array is coded, and retention effects on duration by recoding after the interval is over. The storage size approach can make sense out of duration experience in these many kinds of situations.

Some of the other approaches can account for some of these data, so, as I just stated, all theories are 'true' to some extent. But the storage size approach to duration experience can account for all the effects of the 'biological clock', and all the data of the previous cognitive approaches as well as that of the time-order effect and the results of recoding an experience after the interval. On these two grounds, those of parsimony and those of integrating a wider variety of data than other approaches, the storage approach seems the most useful.

In addition, this approach seems useful in guiding research. It has led inquiry into a new influence on time experience, those of effects on the duration experience of an interval *after* the interval is over.

So, after we have whittled the beginning question down and down, we have an answer to one aspect of one variety of time, that of the experience of duration. This experience seems most usefully considered to be formed from our memories of our experiences. By considering duration to be a construction formed from the size of storage of the information in a given interval, we found that we could make some sense out of 'the wide variety of explanations which have been offered for the time mystery' (Nichols, 1891). We then *create* our own duration experience from our memories.

Some Future Directions

Again, the choice of direction. There are several paths that the storage size analysis leads us to explore. First, and most theoretically relevant, are other effects of retention on time experience. We might try, for instance, to perform the reverse of the 'man' experiment and attempt to *increase* the size of storage of an interval after it is over. We might also consider some procedures which have direct effects on retention of a given interval, perhaps some drugs (in animals) which impair consolidation.

We might more directly alter the storage of an interval by hypnosis. A post-hypnotic suggestion might be given to 'forget' the events of an interval, obtain a duration judgement and remove the suggestion and obtain another judgement.

There are many other kinds of after-interval experiences which might be studied. I will give one example close to ordinary experience. When one leaves a familiar situation and goes away for a while (as in leaving the office routine and going on vacation), when he is about to return it seems as if he had been away for a 'long' time. Yet, on return (to the office) it suddenly seems not to have been 'long' at all. Duration collapses. If you have ever had this type of experience you will know that it is a striking one.

This experience suggests an experiment related to coding processes and duration experience. Harton (1939b) found that 'successful' experiences were estimated as shorter than 'failure' ones. He interpreted his results to show that the more organized an experience, the shorter was duration. In the same way we might view the above example. When one is involved in an experience, one codes it complexly and notes all sorts of possible outcomes of the experience. When the experience is over (when one returns to the office) the whole (vacation) interval becomes coded, chunked over. One remembers, 'We went on vacation' instead of, 'We had a fire, and then went to the beach and . . .'

The experiment, then, would allow some observers to watch or participate in an ongoing event, such as watching a horserace. Just before it is over one would want to stop the race and ask some observers how long it was. Others would be permitted to view the whole race. The prediction would be that those who saw the race *completed* would have experienced it as *shorter* than those who were asked their duration experience near the end, even though the clock time would be *longer* in the case of those who saw the whole race. It is more easily coded for them, complete, while the others have no code, no completion. This approach also suggests that some completed tasks should be judged shorter than incompleted ones.

There are many other kinds of studies which are suggested by the storage size approach, ones not as explicitly related to storage and coding as were the previous experiments. An indication will be given of how the storage size approach handles a few types of experience.

An old saying has it that, 'A watched pot never boils.' Why does it seem so? It seems readily interpretable along storage size lines if we consider that expectancy is a situation which leads to increased sensitivity to stimuli, that as we continually 'watch' the pot, that we are more vigilant than usual. An increase in vigilance should result in a greater amount of awareness of input, and consequently a lengthening of duration experience. But we wouldn't really say that, 'A watched pot *never* boils.' It will boil but it does seem much longer.

In the same way, a 'boring' situation often seems very long to us. Why? In storage size terms this experience could be interpreted this way. Situations which we label 'boring' are ones in which we are forced to attend to more of the stimulus array than we normally would, like listening to a professor drone on and on. Again, an increase in attention, relative to normal experience, would cause a lengthening of duration experience.

Returning to possible experiments, one obvious direction in which to go might be that of attempting a more formal model of duration experience now that a storage size approach is fairly well indicated. No attempt has yet been made to quantitatively relate the amount in storage to duration experience or to hypothesize how storage size might be checked and measured. How much additional experience must there be in storage to lengthen duration experience a given amount? Are the relations between storage size and duration experience additive, monotonic, logarithmic, linear, exponential? The experiments in chapter 4 help little towards building a formal model. They would have been more aid if they were more standardized. Their purpose was not this, however, but rather to poke at the boundaries of the 'mental content' type of cognitive theory and to determine whether specific new variations in input information have a demonstrable effect on duration experience *at all*. The one general quantitative statement which might be made from the results of these studies is that duration experience seems to increase less than linearly with the amount in input, or storage size. In the first study a doubling of the number of stimuli in the interval lengthened duration experience by a factor of about 1·25. Similarly, an increase in complexity of the stimuli in the second experiment from that of four interior angles to eight lengthened duration experience only by a factor of 1·125. The third and fourth studies might provide the basis for more complete parametric variations since the 'randomness' of the random condition, the number of different stimuli, the number of times each stimulus was repeated, all could be varied yielding different amounts of information and a graph could be plotted of this relationship. Even with a comparison of the most redundant possible ordering with the most complex ordering of ten stimuli repeated twenty times each, the experience of duration increases only by a factor of 1·35.

There are some problems with building a quantitative model on this concept since the amount in storage can never really be measured. Additionally, there are many extra-experimental forces at work. When interviewed after an experiment, many observers have stated, in effect, that 'what you psychologists do is to present two equal things and have us say they're different.' Many have confirmed their bias to mark the intervals as 'equal' no matter what they experienced. This mitigates against obtaining useful quantitative data. This also reduces the possibility of obtaining consistent qualitative data. Another problem in obtaining quantitative, rather than just qualitative data is that the magnitude of differences found will be determined by the method of estimation. But this could be standardized.

However, a more precise investigation of the relationship between size of storage and duration experience might be attempted. The data of this study do show some consistency in this regard. In Experiment IX, reducing the number of words used to describe the test stimulus from 73 (uncoded) to 37 (coded 'insect' before interval), reduces the experience of duration again by about 25 per cent. Almost exactly the same result occurred in Experiment VIII. By coding after the interval, the number of words were reduced by $\frac{1}{2}$ again (from 64 to 31) and duration experience was reduced by about 23 per cent. As a beginning statement, one could say that the experience of duration increases less than linearly with the amount in storage, perhaps as a log function of the storage size.

Earlier, we saw that attempts to relate the electrical activity of the brain to time experience were very unsuccessful. They tried to maintain a simple 'tick' of a clock. But there may be a relationship between the EEG and time experience, but not, perhaps one that simple. What might be attempted is to use the EEG as a definition of a mode of information processing and use it to train different modes. The alpha rhythm, though not the 'ticks of a clock', is probably related to a diminution of information processing, a non-response to input. Mulholland and Evans (1966) found alpha to appear when some observers turn their eyes upward, shutting off visual stimuli. It often appears when eyes are shut in general. Cohen (1957), in studying the effects of the ganzfeld, found that some observers would often report a complete absence of visual experience, no sense of vision at all (termed 'blank out'), and that these reports were highly correlated with the appearance of the alpha rhythm in the EEG record. Similarly, Lehmann, Beeler and Fender (1967) found that observers would often report the same experience while viewing a stabilized retinal image and that this experience was also highly correlated with the appearance of alpha waves in the EEG. In an entirely different situation, it has been found that during meditation exercises, Zen (Kasamatsu and Hirai, 1966) and Yoga (Bagchi and Wenger, 1957) practitioners produce large amounts of alpha rhythm. The aim of these meditation practices is, as Behannon (1937) points out, to insulate the practitioner from external stimulation.

We may then assume that alpha rhythms in some way are correlated with a 'turning down' of awareness, of information processing. Kamiya (1962) has shown that observers may be trained to increase their alpha waves *directly*, using the feedback EEG. It would be useful to study time experience during alpha as opposed to non-alpha for a start. One would expect, from the storage size hypothesis, that duration experience in a high alpha state would be shorter than that of, say, in an EEG of arousal, low voltage fast activity. If this study were successful, it might be possible to refine the teaching of autocontrol of cognitive state and teach a slowing of the EEG frequency and determine effects on time experience. We would not be looking for a quantitative relationship between the EEG frequency and the 'ticks' of an unknown clock, but rather an objective means of defining a subjective state of information processing and the subsequent effects of that mode of experience on time experience.

There are many more possible studies generated from this analysis. One might, for instance, want to define more explicitly the differences between short and long time, or to refine the interpretation of the effects of an increase in body temperature on time experience by determining whether cognitive processing does speed up with increasing temperature, but it is more than enough to mention these here now. What is to be concluded is that the storage size approach seems to be a useful way to consider duration experience; it does seem to integrate the data at a useful general level, and has suggested and continues to suggest experiments which further an understanding of duration experience.

References

Adams, J. A. (1964), 'Motor skills', *Ann. Rev. Psychol.*, vol. 202, pp. 181–202.

Astin, A. V. (1968), 'Standards of measurement', *Scient. Amer.*, vol, 218, pp. 50–63.

Attneave, F. (1957),'Physical determinants of the judged complexity of shapes', *J. exper. Psychol.*, vol. 53, pp. 221–7.

Baddeley, A. D. (1966), 'Reduced body temperature and time estimation', *Amer. J. Psychol.*, vol. 79, pp. 475–9.

Bagchi, B. K. and Wenger, M. A. (1957), 'Electro-physiological correlates of some yogi exercises', *EEG clin, Neurophysiol.*, suppl. 7, pp. 132–48.

Bagshaw, M., Kimble, D., and Pribram, K. H. (1965), 'The GSR of monkeys during orienting and habituation and after ablation of the amygdala, hippocampus and inferortemporal cortex', *Neuropsychologica*, vol. 3, pp. 111–19.

Bagshaw, M., and Pribram, J. (1968), 'Effect of amygdalectomy on stimulus threshold of the Monkey', *Exp. Neurology*, vol. 20, pp. 197–202.

Banks, R., and Cappon, D. (1962), 'Effect of reduced sensory input on time perception', *Percep. mot. Skills*, vol. 14, p. 74.

Bartlett, F. C. (1958), *Thinking*, Basic Books.

Behannon, K. (1937), *Yoga, A Scientific Evaluation*, Dover.

Bell, C. R. (1965), 'Time estimation and increases in body temperature', *J. exper. Psychol.*, vol. 70, pp. 232–4.

Bell, C. R., and Provins, K. A. (1963), 'Relation between physiological responses to environmental heat and time judgements', *J. exper. Psychol.* vol. 66, pp. 572–9.

Benussi, V. (1907), 'Zur experimentellen Anakyse des Zeitvergleichs', *Arch. ges. Psychol.*, vol. 9, pp. 384–5.

Bergson, H. (1920), *Essai sur les Donees immediates de la Conscience*, Alcan, 19th edn.

Bergson, H. (1922), *Duration and Simultaneity*, (Bobbs-Merrill edn.) 1965).

Blakey, J. (1934), The discrimination of short empty temporal interval. Unpublished manuscript, as quoted in H. Woodrow. 'The temporal indifference interval determined by the method of mean error', *J. exper. Psychol.*, vol. 17 (1934), pp. 167–88.

Bradley, P. B., and Elkes, J. (1959), 'The effects of some drugs on the electrical activity of the brain', *Exper. Neurol.*, vol. 1, pp. 556–61.

Braitenberg, V., and Onesto, N. (1960), 'The cerebellar cortex as a timing organ', *Sco. intern. Med.*, Cibern, Napoli, pp. 239–55.

Bromberg, W. (1934), 'Marijuana intoxication', *Amer. J. Psychiat.*, vol. 14, pp. 372–7.

Bruner, J. (1957), 'On perceptual readiness', *Psychol. Rev.*, vol. 64, pp. 123–52.

Bünning, E. (1963), *The Physiological Clock*, Springer-Verlag.

Clay, J. (1890), As quoted in W. James, *The Principles of Psychology*, Dover edn, 1950.

Cohen, W. (1957), 'Spatial and textural characteristics of the ganzfeld', *Amer. J. Psychol.* vol. 70, pp. 403–10.

Creelman, C. D. (1962), 'Human discrimination of auditory duration', *J. acoust. Soc. Amer.*, vol. 34, pp. 582–93.

Delay, P. *et al.* (1967), 'Les Champignons hallucinogens dux Mexique as quoted in R. Fischer', *Interdisciplinary perspectives of time*, *Ann. NY Acad. Sci.*, vol. 138 (1967), art. 2.

Dewson, J. H. III, Nobel, K. W., and Pribram, K. H. (1966), 'Corticofugal influence at cochlear nucleus of the cat: Some effects of ablation of insular-temporal cortex', *Brain Res.*, vol. 2, pp. 151–9.

Dimond, S. J. (1964), 'The structural basis of timing', *Psychol. Bull.* vol. 62, pp. 348–50.

Durrell, L. (1960), *Clea*, Dutton.

Fischer, R. (1966), 'Biological time', in J. T. Fraser, ed., *The Voices of Time*, Brazillier.

Fischer, R. (1967), 'The biological fabric of time', in *Interdisciplinary perspectives of time*, *Ann. NY Acad. Sci.*, vol. 138, art. 2.

Fischer, R. (ed.), (1967), 'Interdisciplinary perspectives of time', *Ann. NY Acad. Sci.*, vol. 138, art. 2.

Fischer, R., Griffin, F., and Liss, F. (1962), 'Biological aspects of time in relation to (model) Psychoses', *Ann. NY Acad. Sci.*, vol. 96, pp. 44–64.

Fox, R. H., Bradbury, P. H., Hampton, I. F. G., and Legg, C. F. (1967), 'Time judgement and body temperature', *J. exper. Psychol*, vol. 75, pp. 88–96.

Fraisse, P. (1956), *Les Structures Rythmiques*, Studia Psychologica, Louvain.

Fraisse, P. (1961), 'L'influence de la duree et del la frequence des changements sur l'estimation de temps', *L'Année Psychol.*, pp. 325–39.

Fraisse, P. (1963). *The Psychology of Time*, Harper & Row.

François, M. (1927), 'Contribution a l'etude du sens du temps: La temperature interne comme facteur du variation de l'appreciation subjective des durees', *L'Annee Psychol.*, pp. 186–204.

Frankenhaeuser, M. (1959), *Estimation of Time, An Experimental Study*, Almqvist and Wiksell.

Fraser, J. T. (ed.), (1966), *The Voices of Time*, Brazillier.

Gardner, W. A. (1935), 'The influence of the thyroid gland on the consciousness of time', *Amer. J. Psychol.*, vol. 47, pp. 698–701.

Garner, W. R. (1966), 'To perceive is to know', *Amer. Psychol.*, vol. 21, pp. 1–11.

Gelpke, R. (1967), 'The biological fabric of time', in R. Fischer, *Interdisciplinary perspectives of time*, *Ann. NY Acad. Sci.*, vol. 138, art. 2.

Goldstone, S., Boardman, W. K., and Lhamon, W. T. (1958), 'Effects of quinal barbitone, dextro-amphetamine and placebo on apparent time', *Brit. J. Psychol.*, vol. 49, pp. 324–28.

Grunbaum, A. (1963), *Philosophical Problems of Space and Time*, Knopf.

Gunn, J. A. (1929), *The Problem of Time*, Allen & Unwin.

Guyau, M. (1890), *La Genese de l'idee de temps*, Alcan.

Hall, G. S., and Jastrow, J. (1886), 'Studies of rhythm', *Mind*, vol. 11, pp. 55–60.

Hamner, K. (1966), 'Experimental evidence for the biological clock', in J. T. Fraser, ed., *The Voices of Time*, Brazillier.

Harton, J. J. (1939a), 'The influence of the degree of unity of organization on the estimation of time', *J. gen. Psychol.*, vol. 21, pp. 25–49.

Harton, J. J. (1939b), 'An investigation of the influence of success and failure on the estimation of time', *J. gen. Psychol.*, vol. 21, pp. 51–62.

Hernández-Peón, R., Scherrer, R. H., and Jouvet, M., (1956), 'Modification of electric activity in the cochlear nucleus during "attention" in unanesthetized cats', *Science*, vol. 123, pp. 331–32.

Hoagland, H. (1933), 'The physiological control of judgements of duration: evidence for a chemical clock', *J. gen. Psychol.* vol. 9, pp. 267–87.

Hoagland, H. (1935), 'Pacemakers in relation to aspects of behavior', *Exper. biol. Mono.*, Macmillan.

Hoagland, H. (1966), 'Some biochemical considerations of time', in J. T. Fraser, (ed.), *The Voices of Time*, Brazillier.

Hulser, C. (1934), As quoted in Woodrow, H. 'The temporal indifference interval determined by the method of mean error', *J. exper. Psychol.*, vol. 17, pp. 167–88.

James, W. (1890), *The Principles of Psychology.* (Dover edn, 1950.)

Kamiya, J. (1962), Conditioned discrimination of the EEG alpha rhythm in humans, *Presented at the Western Psychological Assoc., San Francisco.*

Kant, I. (1956), *Critique of Practical Reason*, 1788. (Liberal Arts Press edn, 1956.)

Kasamatsu, A., and Hirai, I. (1966), 'An electroencephalographic study on the Zen Meditation (Zazen)', *Folia Psychia, Neurol., Joponica.*, vol. 20, no. 4.

Kelly, G. (1955). *The Psychology of Personal Constructs*, 2 vols, Norton.

Key, B. J. (1965), 'Effect of LSD on potentials evoked in the specific sensory pathways', *Brit. med. Bull.*, vol. 21, pp. 30–35.

Kleber, R. J., Lhamon, W. T., and Goldstone, S. (1953), 'Hyperthermia, Hyperthyroidism and time judgement', *J. comp. physiol. Psy.*, vol. 56, pp. 362–5.

Koffka, K. (1935), *Principles of Gestalt Psychology*, Harcourt, Brace.

Köhler, G. (1947), *Gestalt Psychology*, New American Library.

Laurie, P. (1967), *Drugs*, Penguin.

Legg, C. (1967), Metabolism, arousal, and subjective time, *Ph.D. thesis, Cambridge University.*

Lehmann, D., Beeler, G. W., and Fender, D. H. (1967), EEG responses during the observation of stabilized and normal retinal images', *EEG clin. Neurophysiol.*, vol. 22, pp. 136–42.

Le Shan (1952), 'Time orientation and social class', *J. abnorm. soc. Psychol.*, vol. 47, pp. 589–92.

Locke, J. (1689), *An Essay Concerning Human Understanding*, (Dover edn, 1959.)

Loehlin, J. C. (1959), 'The influence of different activities on the apparent length of time', *Psychol. Monogr.*, whole no. 474.

Masters, T., and Houston, J. (1966), *The Varieties of Psychedelic Experience*, Dell.

Matsuda, F. (1966), 'Development of time estimation: Effects of frequency of sounds given during standard time', *Jap. J. Psychol.*, vol. 36, pp. 285–94.

Michon, J. (1967), *Timing in Temporal Tracking*, Institute for Perception RVO TNO Soesterberg, The Netherlands.

Michon, J. (1966), 'Tapping regularity as a measure of perceptual motor load', *Ergonomics*, vol. 9, pp. 401–12.

Miller, G. (1956), 'The magical number 7±2; some limits on our capacity for processing information', *Psychol. Rev.*, vol. 63, pp. 81–97.

Mulholland, T., and Evans, C. R. (1966), 'Ocularmotor function and the alpha activation cycle', *Nature*, vol. 211, pp. 1278–9.

Mundy-Castle, A. C., and Sugarman, L. (1960), 'Factors influencing relations between tapping speed and alpha rhythm', *EEG clin. Neurophysiol.*, vol. 12, pp. 895–904.

Münsterberg, H. (1899), *Beitrage yur experimentellen Psychologie*, Heft 2, Sceheck, Frieburg.

Murphee, O. D. (1954), 'Maximum rates of form perception and the alpha rhythm: an investigation and test of current nerve net theory', *J. exper. Psychol.*, vol. 48, pp. 57–61.

Nakamura, H. (1966), 'Time in Indian and Japanese thought', in J. T. Fraser, ed., *The Voices of Time*, Brazillier, 1966.

Neisser, U. (1967), *Cognitive Psychology*, Appleton-Century-Crofts.

Nichols, H. (1891), 'The psychology of time', *Amer. J. Psychol.*, vol. 3, pp. 453–529.

Ochberg, F. M., Pollack, I. W., and Meyer, E. (1964), 'Correlation of pulse and time judgement', *Percep. mot. Skills*, vol. 19, pp. 861–2.

Ostfeld, A. M. (1961), 'Effects of LSD-25 and JB 318 on tests of visual and perceptual functions in man', *Fed. Proc.*, vol. 20, pp. 876–83.

Peterson, L. R., and Peterson, M. Y. (1959), 'Short-term retention of individual verbal items', *J. exper. Psychol.*, vol. 58, pp. 193–8.

Pribram, K. (1967), 'How the brain controls its input', in *Communication: Concepts and Perspectives*, Spartan.

Pribram, K. H. (1969), 'The neurobehavioral analysis of limbic forebrain mechanisms, revision and progress report', in *Advances in the Study of Behavior*, Academic Press.

Pribram, K. H. (1969b), 'The neurophysiology of remembering', *Sci. Amer.*, Jan.

Pribram, K. H., and Melges, F. T. (1968), 'Emotion: The search for control', in P. J. Vinken and G. W. Bruyn, eds., *Handbook of Clinical Neurology*, North-Holland.

Purpura, D. (1967), 'Neurophysiological actions of LSD', in R. DeBold, ed., *LSD, Man and Society*, Wesleyan University Press.

Roelofs, C. O., and Zeaman, W. P. C. (1951), 'Influence of different sequences of optical stimuli on the estimation of the duration of a given interval of time', *Acta Psychol.*, vol. 8, pp. 89–128.

Saunders, J. (1967), 'As described in "Science and the Citizen"', *Scient. Amer.*, vol. 217, no. 1.

Spinelli, D. N., and Pribram, K. H., (1967), 'Changes in visual recovery functions and unit activity produced by frontal and temporal cortex stimulation', *EEG clin. Neurophysiol.*, vol. 22, pp. 143–9.

Stroud, J. M. (1956), 'The fine structure of psychological time', in H. Quastler, ed., *Information Theory and Psychology*, Free Press.

Stroud, J. M. (1967), 'The fine structure of psychological time', in R. Fischer, ed., *Interdisciplinary perspectives of time*, Ann. *NY Acad. Sci.*, vol. 138, art. 2.

Tichener, E. B. (1905), *Experimental Psychology*, vol. 11, part 2, Macmillan.

Treisman, M. (1963), 'Temporal discrimination and the indifference interval: Implications for a model of the internal clock', *Psychol. Monog.*, vol. 77, whole no. 576.

Vernon, J., and McGill, R. (1963), 'Time estimation during sensory deprivation', *J. gen. Psych.*, vol. 69, pp. 11–18.

Watson, J. B. (1924), *Behaviorism*, (University of Chicago Press edn, 1961.)

White, C. T. (1963), 'Temporal numerosity and the psychological unit of duration', *Psychol. Monogr.*, whole no. 575.

Wiener, N. (1948), *Cybernetics*, Wiley.

Winer, B. J. (1962), *Statistical Principles in Experimental Design*, McGraw-Hill.

Wolfe, T. (1968), *The Electric Kool Aid Acid Test*, Farrar Strauss and Giroux.

Woodrow, H. (1934), 'The temporal indifference interval determined by the method of mean error', *J. exper. Psychol.*, vol. 17, pp. 167–188.

Woodrow, H. (1951), 'Time perception', in S. S. Stevens, ed., *Handbook of Experimental Psychology*, Wiley.

Woodworth, R. S., and Schlosberg, H. (1954), *Experimental Psychology*, Holt.

Wright, R. L. D., and Kennard, M. A. (1957), 'Thresholds of visual recognition and its relation to harmonic EEG responses to flicker', *Canad. J. Psychol.*, vol. 11, pp. 245–52.

Index